THE GIFT OF LOVE

Also by Amy Clipston

THE GIFT OF LOVE

One Woman's Journey to Save a Life

AMY CLIPSTON

ZONDERVAN

The Gift of Love
Copyright © 2013 by Amy Clipston

This title is also available as a Zondervan ebook.
Visit www.zondervan.com/ebooks.

Requests for information should be addressed to:

Zondervan, *Grand Rapids, Michigan* 49530

Library of Congress Cataloging-in-Publication Data

Clipston, Amy.
 A gift of love : one woman's journey to save a life / Amy Clipston.
  pages cm
  ISBN 978-0-310-33134-6 (softcover)
  1. Kidneys—Transplantation—Patients—Biography. 2. Kidneys—Transplantation—Patients—Family relationships. 3. Kidneys—Diseases—Patients—Biography. 4.
 Organ donors—Biography. 5. Transplantation of organs, tissues, etc.—Anecdotes. I. Title.
 RD575.C57 2013
 617.4'610592—dc23   2013033154

Cover design: Curt Diepnhorst
Cover photo: Dan Davis Photography
Photo Stylist: Rita Vogg
Interior design: Katherine Lloyd, The DESK

Printed in the United States of America

14 15 16 17 18 19 /DCI/ 23 22 21 20 19 18 17 16 15 14 13 12 11 10 9 8 7 6 5 4 3 2 1

For Jeanne and Stacey,
who saw me at my worst but didn't abandon me.

✌

For my mother-in-law, Sharon,
for her unwavering support.

✌

And also for my mother, Lola Goebelbecker.
Mom, words can't express how much I appreciate
all you do for our family.
You're my rock. I love you!

CONTENTS

THE GIFT OF LOVE

Chapter One

SOMEONE LOOKING OUT FOR ME

"I NEED TO TALK TO JOE. I'VE BEEN HIT." I pleaded with my mother to get my husband to come to the phone. My hands shook, mirroring the terror surging through me. "Can you get Joe? I've been hit!"

"Oh, no! Wait, wait. Hang on. I'll get Joe." My mother's voice was filled with worry. "Just a minute." I heard her yell his name and I imagined her standing at the bottom of the stairs, gazing up toward where our bedroom was. "Joe! Pick up the phone! It's Amy. It's an emergency."

She returned, her voice overwrought. "He's coming. What happened? Are you all right?"

"A semi hit me," I said, tears streaming down my hot cheeks. "Can you believe it, Mom? It was a semi!" My tongue felt as if it had swollen to twice its size and it hurt to speak. Pain shot through my leg and I wondered if it was broken. But I was in one piece! I was still alive!

"Oh, no." My mom's usual loud and confident voice quavered. "He's coming. Just hold on."

The phone line clicked as Joe picked up an extension. "Yeah?" He sounded wide awake even though it was only six o'clock in the morning.

"I got hit!" I began a rant about the accident. "I was hit by a semi. You have to come. You need to come *now*."

"Slow down." Joe's calm tone did little to relieve my panic. "Where are you?"

The question was simple, but I was dumbstruck. I'd driven this route, a straight shot northwest from Union County to Uptown Charlotte, to and from work for the past two years. Yet I had no earthly idea where I was. I looked up at the street sign on the corner above my smashed 2005 Ford Escape and found myself momentarily illiterate. A renewed panic surged through me.

"I don't know where I am." Confused tears clouded my vision. "I don't know where I am!"

Several minutes earlier, I had been on my way to the park and ride, located at a shopping center approximately four miles from my home. I had been driving down Route 74, also known as Independence Boulevard in this location, a four-lane congested highway that is a main artery for trucks and cars headed from Charlotte to the coast. On any given day, thundering packs of tractor trailers could be spotted making the trek down Route 74. I hadn't given the behemoth vehicles much thought until that fateful day of April 30, 2008.

After exiting my neighborhood that morning, I merged onto Route 74 and sang along (albeit off-key) with Mark Wills's hit country song "19 Somethin'." When it was safe, I signaled and maneuvered into the right lane to prepare to turn into the park-and-ride lot located in the Food Lion parking lot just past the intersection at Sardis Church Road.

The light at the intersection turned red and I came to a stop. And that's when it happened. Looking into my rearview mirror, I found the jarring reflection of an eighteen-wheeler bearing down on me. I gripped the steering wheel as I realized the monstrous truck wasn't decelerating. I thought, "He's not stopping."

Now, when I think of that moment, it feels as though the accident occurred in slow motion. Stop-motion images fill my mind. The semi slamming into the back of my little Ford Escape ... The rear window shattering ... The tractor-trailer's engine filling my vehicle with the snarling growl of a massive predator devouring its tiny, defenseless prey ...

As my SUV plunged forward toward the rear of the other eighteen-wheeler, icy tendrils of fear gripped my spine. "This is it," I thought as I stared at the reflector tape on the bumper of the semi in front of me. "I'm going to die and I'll never see my boys again."

And then everything accelerated and my Escape hurtled forward with the speed of a racecar, crashing into the bumper of the other semi.

I imagine the force of my little SUV hitting that gargantuan truck was similar to a pebble hitting its windshield, but the impact knocked me out cold or I blacked out from the horror because I don't remember the moment at all. All I know is that by some miracle my Escape didn't cross the center lane and collide with oncoming traffic or plunge into a nearby ditch. Instead, my vehicle simply came to a stop in the shoulder, away from other commuters. It was as if the hand of God had retrieved my little SUV and gently placed it on the side of the road.

When I regained my awareness, I heard an unfamiliar voice shrieking. It took me a few moments to realize the strange, hysterical voice was my own. The pitch and loudness of my voice embodied the terror that had consumed me the moment the semi rammed into my SUV's rear bumper and shattered the glass in the tailgate.

I managed to curb my screams, which then allowed me to focus on the *pain*. Oh, such pain! Lightning bursts of agony shot through my right femur. My back and neck also hurt, but the feeling in my leg overshadowed any other discomfort. I was certain it had been broken, and tears flooded my eyes.

"Where are you?" Joe's voice rang through the phone, bringing me back to reality.

I looked out the window and spotted the driver of the semi my SUV had hit. He was walking toward me in confusion, as if he wasn't sure what on earth had happened. I was thrilled to see this stranger. He could act as the GPS to guide my husband to me. I needed Joe to save the day!

I opened the window as he approached.

"Are you okay?" the man asked.

"I don't know." I shoved my cell phone toward him. "Can you tell my husband where I am?" He looked at me and then at the phone, which I shook at him. "Please!"

Bemused, the truck driver took the phone. He explained

to Joe where we were, then handed the phone back to me. I thanked him before putting the phone to my ear. "Hurry!" I instructed Joe. "I need you here."

"I'll be there as soon as I can," Joe promised before disconnecting the call.

Traffic on Route 74 was backed up, thanks to my accident, and it seemed like a lifetime before I spotted Joe's black Suburban parked on the other side of the highway. Relief flooded me when he approached with a Union County sheriff in tow. "Are you okay?" Joe asked.

"My leg hurts. I think it's broken." My eyes filled with more frustrated tears. "And my back and neck hurt."

"The ambulance is on its way," the sheriff assured me.

I studied Joe's expression as his eyes moved over my poor SUV. As I watched his expression, alarm filled me. I knew it was bad, really bad.

"Is it totaled?" I asked, my voice shaking like a child awaiting punishment.

"Yeah." Joe nodded for emphasis. "It's totaled all right."

Panic gripped me as I looked at the sheriff. "We can't afford a car!" I blurted. "He needs a kidney transplant!"

Joe shook his head and looked as if he didn't know if he should laugh or remain serious. "Don't worry about that right now. It'll be okay."

The sheriff seemed stunned as he studied me. I realized much later that it was ridiculous of me to worry about affording a new car after my SUV was crunched by a semi. After all, that's why drivers — and, in this situation, trucking companies — are required to have insurance.

The sheriff told me to wait in the vehicle for the ambulance. Soon we heard the sirens blaring in the distance as the ambulance wove through the bottlenecked traffic. When it arrived, one of the two emergency medical technicians asked me what parts of my body were in pain. I explained my leg was the biggest problem, but as soon as I mentioned back and neck pain, they brought out the dreaded wooden backboard. I'm convinced this contraption is used as a form of torture. Not only was it awkward and complicated for the two EMTs to remove me from the SUV and place me onto the board, but it was horribly uncomfortable.

Once I was loaded onto the gurney, I said goodbye to Joe, who promised to come to the hospital.

Much later, Joe told me the truck driver that had hit me approached him after the EMTs took me away in the ambulance. The driver asked Joe if we had any children. When Joe responded yes, the driver broke down and sobbed. Hearing that, I was touched by his remorse about the accident. Although he'd made a mistake that could have been tragic, he was penitent. And, as crazy as it may sound, that warmed my heart.

I never found out why his semi had crushed my SUV. Perhaps he'd fallen asleep after a long haul, or maybe he was searching for a radio station. I'll never know what caused it, but I know in my heart he was truly contrite.

During the agonizing ride to the hospital, I stared at the ceiling of the ambulance and wondered if my accident was being reported on the radio. I imagined the traffic reporter announcing, "A three-vehicle accident involving two tractor trailers has traffic down to one lane westbound on Independence Boulevard in Union County by Sardis Church Road. Drivers should consider using an alternate route, such as Old Monroe Road." I wondered how many people were late for work due to my mishap that morning. I wondered if my friends and colleagues were.

We arrived at the emergency room and the EMTs wheeled me into a treatment room, where I was moved onto a bed while still attached to the torturous board. Joe sat in a chair beside my bed. I was thankful that my thoughtful husband had taken care of all of the calls I needed him to make for me before he arrived at the hospital. Joe had called my mother to tell her I seemed okay but was at the hospital for an exam. He'd found my boss's number in my cell phone and called to tell him I would be out for at least a couple of days. He'd also connected with his parents and told them about the accident. Knowing he had done these things for me — that he had worked to allay the concerns he knew I'd have — made me love him all the more.

A radiology technician came to retrieve me and steered the gurney down a busy hallway toward the radiology room. The tall man dressed in scrubs had an amiable face and a soothing voice. He asked me what had happened, and I detailed the accident.

He shook his head and then pointed to the lapel on my brown suit jacket. "Someone was looking out for you."

Confused, I glanced down and spotted an angel pin that a dear friend at my former job in Norfolk, Virginia, had given me. I hadn't remembered I was wearing the pin until the man pointed it out. Warmth filled me at the thought of someone protecting me during that accident.

I smiled up at him. "Yes, I think you're right." Someone *had* been looking out for me. I knew I survived that accident through more than just dumb luck. It was divine intervention. An angel or God himself had saved me.

And that was when I began to pray. With my eyes closed and the MRI machine humming around me, I thanked God over and over again for saving me from that accident, for gifting me with two darling sons, for blessing me with a loving husband, and for giving me all of the joys in my life — my home, my parents, my cats, my job, everything. I repeated this prayer over and over again until the MRI was complete.

I cannot explain the relief that flooded me when the nurse told me that my back, neck, and leg weren't broken and I could finally get up from the backboard and go to the restroom. Resembling a zombie, I staggered on rubber legs across the length of the room toward the restroom. A man sitting in the treatment area next to me stared as if I'd just announced I was visiting from Mars.

"What happened to you?" He squinted up at me from a rickety chair.

"I was hit by a semi," I muttered. I didn't wait for his reaction or further questions. Instead, I continued to schlep past him and found the bathroom in the hallway.

When I finally stood in front of the mirror, I gasped at my haggard reflection. I truly did resemble a zombie! My hair was bedraggled and sticking out in all directions. My clothing was disheveled. Dried blood outlined my lips. I opened my mouth, stuck out my tongue, and found the source of the blood — the left side of my tongue was purple and swollen. I didn't remember the impact, so I assumed I had bitten down on my tongue when my SUV smashed into the semi in front of it.

I studied my expression. The fear and pain etched on my face made me look as if I had physically taken a blow from the accident. Images returned — the truck, the smashing of glass ...

Shaking, I grabbed a paper towel and cleaned the blood off my face and then tried to fix my hair by finger-combing it. Once I'd done what I could, I used the restroom and then returned to my treatment area, where I glared at Joe.

"Why didn't you tell me I had blood all around my mouth?" I snapped.

His eyes widened. "I didn't notice it."

Such a man response. "You should've told me. It looked gross. No wonder everyone was staring."

To that Joe had no response. Thankfully, the doctor took that moment to return. He explained my back and neck were only suffering with whiplash, and he gave me a prescription for a painkiller. He also told me that my painful leg wasn't broken and he suggested I use ice on my femur where a large hematoma had developed. He suggested Popsicles for my painful tongue. "You should take it easy for the rest of the week," he said.

After a flurry of paperwork, I was freed. Joe and I headed home as I called my mother to tell her I was fine and would be there soon. She sounded relieved.

At home, I rested on the sofa in my mother's suite with ice on my throbbing leg and a Popsicle soothing my swollen tongue. I was thankful to be there. Images and sounds haunted my thoughts, but I focused on the positive — I was alive and in one piece. I could walk, despite the hematoma on my leg and the soreness in my back and neck. I was going to make it. Like the MRI technician said, the Lord had been looking out for me.

I believed that then and I believe it now. That accident was one of the most terrifying moments of my life, but I'm certain God's angels protected me. I'm also certain one of the reasons I walked away from it all was so I could donate a kidney for my husband three years later. God needed my kidneys, and he kept them safe.

Chapter Two

PEN PALS,
PREPS, AND PEPSI

MY FATHER, LUDWIG "BOB" GOEBELBECKER, WAS a German immigrant who came to the United States with his mother and his two older siblings in 1929 when he was nine months old. My grandfather had come to the United States several months earlier to find a job before sending for my grandmother. They first landed in the German section of New York City, then settled in New Jersey.

Like many families before and after them, they had immigrated in hopes of finding a better life. According to my father, back then the United States was advertised like a paradise where streets were paved in gold. It wasn't quite that easy, of course. There were lots of adjustments — not the least being the language barrier. Neither of my grandparents spoke English when they arrived, so they learned the language by listening to the radio. My grandmother even kept her oldest child, my uncle Emil, home from school an extra year in order to give him the opportunity to learn English.

My grandparents worked as superintendents in an apartment building during the day, and at night my grandfather worked as an ironworker designing railings. I was always in awe of their bravery in moving alone to a new country with young children when they were only in their twenties. Still, despite their courage, they struggled. We treasure a photo of their first Christmas in the United States. In the photograph, no one is smiling, and on the back of the print, my nana wrote, "So homesick."

My mother, Lola, who was ten years younger than my father, grew up in Paterson, New Jersey, as the daughter of a single mother. My mother's parents divorced when she was two years old and her brother, Joe, was four. Lola spent her childhood living in low-income apartments and had to quit school in eighth grade to get a job and help pay rent.

My grandmother worked in a laundry, where she folded sheets as they came off the mangle. Since my grandmother never learned to drive, my mother remembers walking six blocks in the dark every morning to go to her grandparents' house before school. Her mother would then walk another ten blocks to work.

My mother grew up in a "cold-water flat," which means there was no running hot water, and all of the water had to be boiled. The apartment was heated with a large coal stove in the kitchen, and the bathroom was located outside the apartment in the hallway. The rent was $13.80 per month.

Every Saturday morning, my mother and grandmother would walk approximately ten blocks to the courthouse to retrieve a child support check from my mother's absentee father. Mom only remembers meeting her father twice before he passed away when she was eleven.

My parents met through mutual friends when my mother was nineteen and my father was twenty-nine. You could say it was love at first sight since they were engaged after only three months. They lived in Paterson when they were first married. Back then, my father was in the New Jersey National Guard full-time, and my mother worked at a dry cleaners.

Although she never finished high school, my mother has more common sense than most folks I've met with graduate degrees. While I was growing up, she worked as a school guard for the local police department and also babysat in our home. Her income paid for extras in our family, such as vacations to Schroon Lake in Pottersville, New York, and trips to Disney World in Florida.

It was to these two amazing people that I was born, along with my older brother, Eric. We grew up in Ridgewood, New Jersey, a middle- to upper-middle-class town in northeastern New Jersey, not far from New York City. Ours was the quintessential American home, a cottage built in the 1920s complete with a white picket fence and a rose trellis. It sat high on a hill overlooking a small cul-de-sac.

My bedroom was up on the second floor. Although it wasn't much larger than ten by ten, it was a penthouse in my eyes, my kingdom and my hideaway. I blasted my favorite music on my stereo, and I tirelessly penned silly stories in notebooks and wrote hundreds of letters to pen pals around the world. Throughout my school years, pen pals were a wonderful way for me to connect with girls who shared my interest in music, movies, and books. For many years, I kept a special box bursting with my letters. Some of my pen pals wrote to me weekly or even daily. I loved the escape that letter writing provided me.

Another form of escape for me was our huge backyard. With the help of my active imagination, I would magically transform the yard into a baseball stadium or a jungle for safaris. My best friend Christine lived down the street. If we weren't playing with our Barbie dolls or riding bikes, we were playing outside.

These days were also a time of figuring out how I fit into the grand scheme of things. Our land formed the line for the neighboring town, Midland Park. On the other side of Ridgewood was an area we called "the heights," where the preppie (popular) kids lived in their mini-mansions and rode in their flashy European cars. Most of them received brand-new cars on their seventeenth birthday.

I quickly figured out in elementary school that I was never going to fit in with the preps. In sixth grade, however, the reality of my place in the social spectrum was driven home to me.

I was in a class and a group of us were joking around while playing Mad Libs. Everyone was laughing and teasing each other in good fun.

When it came my turn to say a noun, I looked at one of the popular boys sitting near me and said, "Collared shirt," in reference to the shirt he was wearing.

The boy glared at me and said, "My shirt is worth more than your house. I know where you live."

I was humiliated and crushed by his cruel words. With all of the laughing and camaraderie in the classroom, I had thought we were possibly friends, but his words cut me to the bone and instantly put me in my place.

In an attempt to defend my beloved little home I said, "Maybe my house is big enough for my family."

The boy didn't respond to me. The class continued playing Mad Libs, but I could no longer concentrate on the game. I silently stewed on his mean words. I knew my retort had been meaningless, and I was already labeled one of the poor kids no matter how much I tried to defend my home. To this day, I remember the humiliation of that moment.

After that, I gave up trying to fit in with the popular kids and decided to embrace my individuality. I became the opposite of the preps. When Coke apparel was popular in middle school, I purchased Pepsi sweatshirts and smiled when a popular girl informed me that Pepsi was wimpy. I avoided all of the latest styles and overpriced clothes. I discovered music from the 1960s and drowned my feelings of inadequacy in the lyrics of the Beatles, Monkees, Mamas and Papas, and other bands.

My father accused me of becoming a reverse snob when I turned my nose up at the latest styles or snooty name brands. I know he was right; to this day I still do my best to avoid the overpriced clothing lines and stores that remind me of the shallow, arrogant kids who hurt my feelings back in Ridgewood.

At the time my deepest wish was to start a new life where I could reinvent myself and be "the new girl." My dream came true when I graduated from high school. In June 1991 my father retired at age sixty-two, and we moved to Virginia Beach, Virginia.

We loved it there—with its beautiful oceanfront, friendly shopping centers, and affordable living. My parents built their dream house—a ranch style with a big room over the garage for me—in a brand-new planned development named Pine Meadows. I was in heaven with my new, bigger hideaway. It had slanted ceilings that I covered in posters, just as I had done in my house in Ridgewood.

We settled into our new life. I lived at home and commuted to Virginia Wesleyan College. During my second year at college, I declared communications as my major, the umbrella for public relations, journalism, and broadcasting. After seeing my parents struggle to stay afloat all my life, I was thankful to be the first person in my immediate family to attend college.

Commuting to school sometimes made my life difficult socially. I found friends through a few clubs and activities and even tried joining a sorority for a year. But I worked hard in college and took my courses seriously. I quickly figured out that the students who only wanted to party weren't the scholarship kids like me.

Between classes I went to my work-study job at the college's media relations office. Thanks to a wonderful supervisor who took me under her wing, I grew to love public relations and dreamt of working in the field. I became the first student editor of *DayOne*, the college newsletter, and I instituted weekly editions. I also learned how to write press releases and worked on the college magazine. Life was good.

Chapter Three

THE DAY
EVERYTHING CHANGED

ALTHOUGH HE NEVER COMPLETED HIS BACHELOR'S degree, my father was the smartest man I ever knew. He sold industrial-strength filters for Process Equipment and Supply Company located in Jersey City, New Jersey. He had an infectious sense of humor and a love of music. Although he was forty-three when I was born, he seemed like a young father to me. Some of my favorite memories were of him watching *Headbangers Ball*, a heavy-metal music program on MTV, and also seeing him dance outside his car while blasting "Funkytown" through the speakers.

Dad had a deep love and appreciation for our family history and was proud of his German heritage. In 1986 we traveled to Germany to visit my brother Eric, who was stationed there in the army. We shopped, enjoyed German food, and toured a host of castles. We also met many of my father's relatives, and stayed in Dettenheim, his birthplace, with my father's cousins. There we visited a historic church that held marriage and baptism records for my family dating back to the 1700s. My father said he felt a connection to the village, even though he had left it in his infancy.

He felt a connection to Virginia Beach as well. Our new home was Dad's paradise. Since Mom was still working full-time, he took over at home, doing yard work, grocery shopping, and cleaning. He had a schedule taped on the back of a cabinet in his brand-new kitchen. Mondays he grocery shopped, Tuesdays he cleaned the bathrooms, and so on.

Although my father had diabetes and high blood pressure, he was otherwise healthy. He loved yard work and spent hours outside. We had the most beautiful lawn in the community. At night, neighbors walking past would stop and touch the grass to see if it was real. Mom always joked, "It's the color of money," referring to the amount of cash Dad spent at the home improvement store to make the lawn so inviting.

All my life, but especially while I was in college, my father was my buddy. When I was young, I called him a walking encyclopedia because he had a tidbit of information for any subject. As I grew older I came to appreciate his depth of knowledge. We enjoyed talking about books, and he'd help me study for class. He even helped me with German. He was such a part of my everyday life.

But all that changed on April 30, 1994. When I spoke to my father before I left for class that day, he sounded strange and his words were slurred. I was concerned, but I went to class anyway.

Later in the day I called him from my work-study job, hoping and praying he would sound normal again. He still didn't sound like himself. In fact, it was as if he was speaking through a mouthful of marbles. I had no idea what was wrong with him and couldn't understand a word he was saying. It worried me, but in my ignorance I assumed he'd be fine. Surely it was something minor.

After classes that day I went shopping with my big sister from the sorority and her mother. I kept thinking about my father and wondering how he was. My heart wasn't in our shopping trip, but I was trapped in my friend's mom's minivan with no way to get in touch with my parents — these were the days before cell phones. A voice in the back of my head kept telling me to go home, but I continued moving from store to store with my friend and her mother.

Later that evening, we returned to my friend's home. Her mother checked the answering machine and then called for me. "Amy, come quickly. Your mother left a message."

"This message is for Amy. This is her mother. I need to get in touch with her right away." My mother's overwrought voice rang through the machine, and I knew immediately that something was wrong. "I think your father has had a stroke. I'm taking him to Beach General. I need you to come right away. Meet me at the hospital as soon as you can."

The answering machine clicked off, and I felt as if the world had been tilted on its axis. This couldn't possibly be happening to me. How could my father have a stroke? He was my strong daddy who took care of everything. He protected us. He was my buddy!

I found out later that my mother had gone home early from work and discovered my father in bed. She spent the afternoon trying to convince him to go to the hospital but wasn't successful until later in the day. She was frustrated when she couldn't reach me, and I felt so incredibly guilty when I found out she'd needed my help. I wished I could rewind time in order to go home and help her take care of my father.

But I couldn't. And from that point on everything changed. My father walked into the hospital the day of his stroke, but he didn't walk out. The stroke was massive, leaving his right side paralyzed and his words slurred. He had to relearn how to walk, and he had to take speech therapy. We were devastated by the instant change in him. He'd been a strong, intelligent man, and overnight he was reduced to someone who had to learn how to tie his shoes with only one hand.

Not only that, but the essence of my father changed that day. Gone was my buddy, replaced by someone I didn't know. At the emergency room he was agitated. He glared up at my mother, venom dripping from his voice as he accused her, "You brought me here." He had no concept of what had happened and why he was there. It broke my heart.

That night I called my brother in New Jersey, crying as I shared the news. I felt as if my life was falling apart and nothing would ever be the same for our family. Even retired, my father was the head of our family. He was our leader. Now he was handicapped and confused, unable to do anything without assistance.

The new direction of our lives hit home the very next day. That morning, I was inducted into the National Honor Society.

I was so proud, but I longed to have my father at the special event. After all, I was the first in my immediate family to attend college, and I had worked hard enough to earn this distinction. Instead of enjoying this honor, however, I worried about him and wondered about the long-term impacts on his health. I sensed my life and my mother's life had been changed forever by my father's massive stroke.

After a week's stay at Virginia Beach General Hospital, Dad was moved to a rehabilitation facility a few blocks away. My mother and I went to visit him, and I was stunned at the man I found there. He was no longer my brilliant, confident father. Instead, he was a shell of the man I used to know and admire. He could barely walk or talk. He seemed confused when we spoke to him. I said something to him in German, and he tilted his head and stared at me with confusion. He was emotional and weepy, and he cried when his roommate, a cranky elderly man, was released to go home.

I was heartsick. Who was this stranger? Where was the father I'd known and loved my whole life? The change in him was overwhelming, and I mourned all that he'd lost. He had only enjoyed three years of his hard-earned retirement before he was rendered handicapped. Now he wouldn't get to take the trips he'd dreamt about or finish the projects he wanted to do around the house. Instead, he had to learn how to put on his socks with the aid of a metal holder.

Doctors told Mom that Dad would be lucky if he learned to dress himself and write his name. But Dad eventually did defy the odds. After four weeks in the rehab facility, he came home. Soon he proved himself able to take care of the laundry and mow the lawn, even with the use of only one hand. Of course, the tasks took him longer to do, but he was determined to still contribute to the family.

Although physically Dad regained some of his old abilities, emotionally he wasn't the same man my mother and I had known. Dad was now more difficult to live with. He was short-tempered and critical of my mother. She couldn't even measure out the water for his oatmeal according to his standards. He would stand behind her and remeasure the water when she walked away.

I know now his difficult personality was caused by his own frustrations with his handicap. He told my mother, "I used to be in charge of everything, but now I'm in charge of nothing." At the time, however, I couldn't tolerate how he treated my mother. My blood would boil every time he criticized her.

One night my mother approached me while I was sitting on my bed studying for a test. I could tell by her expression that it was serious. "I think we need to talk."

"What's up?" I asked as I leaned back against a pillow.

Standing in the doorway, she said, "You need to learn to let some things go when it comes to your father. I know you think you're defending me when he's nasty, but when you interfere you actually make it worse. He gets even more agitated and everything escalates from there. You have to be patient with him even though it's difficult."

I shook my head. "I can't stand it when he talks to you like that. You're the one working full-time, chauffeuring him to doctor's appointments, taking care of the household, and taking care of him. He needs to appreciate you more. He's disrespectful."

She smiled. "Thank you for saying that, but he doesn't really mean what he says. He's frustrated by how the stroke changed him, and he's just taking his frustrations out on me."

"It's not right."

Mom's exhaustion reflected in her eyes. "I know it isn't right, but this is our life now. We just have to accept it."

"Okay." I nodded. "I'll try to stay out of it."

"Thank you."

As she disappeared down the stairs, I contemplated her words. I knew in my heart that she was right and I needed to respect her request even though it was pure torture for me to stand by and watch my father castigate my mother. I had to try my best to stay out of my parents' business and let her handle their arguments in her own way.

My father's change went deeper than just his temperament. His personality transformed overnight. He was often confused, at times not able to think of words he wanted to say. Before the stroke, he had loved to discuss politics, and he would trap anyone who would listen while he rambled on about his opinion of the world. It used to drive me crazy, especially when he would entice my friends into lengthy conversations. I despised politics because I heard about it endlessly at home.

After the stroke, however, I missed the political rants. To this day, I long to hear my father's point of view of the country and the world. I would give anything to ask him about current events. It's funny how you miss things when they're gone. Although my father survived his stroke, I'd lost the man who raised me, and I missed him desperately.

This new life took a toll on me. I fell into a deep depression, crying constantly and moping around the house feeling sorry for myself and my family. I slept in my parents' room because I didn't want to be alone.

One afternoon my then boyfriend appeared at my house unexpectedly. I opened the front door. "I didn't know you were coming over."

"Your mom called me and asked me to get you out of the house."

"My mother called you?" I glanced behind me while searching for my sneaky mother. "What did she say?"

"She's worried about you because you've been moping around the house ever since your dad had the stroke. She said you needed to get out. So let's go."

"Okay." I called toward the kitchen, "I'm heading out."

"Have fun!" Mom replied with a wave.

"Where are we going?" I couldn't stop my smile as I followed him to his truck. Mom was right; I needed to get out. I was thankful that she knew me so well.

"We're going to Joe's."

"Really?" Excitement filled me. "I'm finally going to meet your friends?"

"Yes, you are," he said as we climbed into the truck. "Hopefully, they'll all be over there."

I had been bugging him to introduce me to the friends he discussed constantly. That day he finally took me to the "hangout spot" — which happened to be my future husband's parents' house.

Chapter Four

A New Last Name

I HAD NO IDEA MY LIFE WOULD BE forever changed when I walked into a strange house and met Joseph Clipston. He was sitting on the sofa watching television when my current boyfriend and I entered. Although I was normally nervous around dogs, I quickly made friends with the family dog, Spike. Soon I was sitting on the floor petting Spike, who relaxed and seemed happy for the attention.

The first words Joe said to me were: "You're spoiling my dog."

How's that for a romantic meeting?

Still, there was something about this young man that drew me. I learned Joe worked full-time in a body shop at a car dealership and had been in a relationship with the same girl for five-and-a-half years. (I arbitrarily wondered if I would last that long with my current boyfriend.) I also found out Joe's father had recently had a heart attack, so we had some common ground.

Over the next couple of months, I became close to my boyfriend's sister — who also was friends with Joe's family — and we frequented their house, often without her brother. I liked hanging out there. My girlfriend had grown up with Joe and his friends, and they were like a family. Joe's friends were funny and welcoming. We spent most of our time together talking and laughing, which was a nice relief from the atmosphere in my home. I related to my new friends more than I did to most of my acquaintances at college. Since Joe and his friends were working-class people like my parents, I felt at home around them.

Most of all, I enjoyed getting to know Joe. He was easy to talk to, and we fell into deep conversations about everything from our families to life in general. I realized Joe was a hard worker and a car nut. He always had a car project going. His favorite cars were AMC Gremlins, and he enjoyed replacing the stock engines with V8s. He bragged about street-racing his Gremlin against a Corvette and beating it.

In June, my boyfriend's sister tearfully shared that her brother had been cheating on me. All of the signs had been apparent, but I was young, naïve, and too trusting. Looking back, it was obvious he wasn't truly working all the time, and he also had put away my framed photo that was on his dresser in his apartment because he was "dusting." (What guy dusts?)

I broke up with the guy, and I was hurt. Mostly, I was disappointed in myself for not seeing the obvious signs he was cheating. But I also knew all was not lost. In fact, I had learned a lot, and I came out of the relationship smarter and more confident.

I continued to spend time at Joe's parents' house. And I quickly developed a crush on Joe.

One night the phone rang at my house, and I answered it in the kitchen.

"Hey. I just got home from work a little while ago. It was a long day. It's been really busy." A familiar masculine voice chattered on to me about his day. I had no idea who he was, but I was too embarrassed to admit it and ask his name. "My dad is working late and my mom is out," he continued. "Jason just left with his girlfriend. I was just sitting here watching television."

"Oh." I smiled, thankful to have figured out it was Joe when he mentioned his brother, Jason. "That's what I was just doing too."

"Do you like to go to the beach?" he asked.

"Yes."

"I like to go up to Sandbridge. Sometimes I just drive around out there."

"That's nice." An awkward moment of silence passed between us. Finally, I mustered all of my confidence and asked, "Are you asking me to go for a ride with you?"

"Yes."

"Well, then, come pick me up."

That evening we spent hours driving around Sandbridge Beach and pointing out the houses we liked. I was surprised our architectural tastes were similar, and I was also surprised by how comfortable I felt with Joe. Conversation with him was easy. I could be myself and not have to try to impress him. My feelings for him deepened, and I hoped our friendship would blossom into something more.

Joe and his girlfriend broke up, and he and I began spending time together regularly that summer. One night we sat on the hood of a car in his parents' driveway and talked. Hours flew past as we discussed everything from cars to our hopes and dreams. I knew then that I'd finally found my soul mate — the one person who truly understood and cared about me. He was the sounding board and friend I needed during that difficult time. I was thankful our paths had crossed.

Joe was also my strength as my mother and I adjusted to life after my father's stroke. For several months after the stroke, our lives were in turmoil at home, and I often felt lost without my father's strong emotional support. Joe would patiently listen to me talk about my dad and how much he had changed. The grief of losing the father I'd known all my life was overwhelming, but Joe helped me through it.

That summer was a whirlwind and I ran on the adrenaline of new love. I could steal two hours of sleep and still function at my internship working on the features desk at the *Virginian-Pilot* newspaper in Norfolk. Joe and I spent our weekends at Oregon Inlet in the Outer Banks of North Carolina. We would pack a picnic lunch and drive out onto the beach, watching the waves and talking. Evenings during the week we talked in the driveway or cruised around town.

My mother and my best friend at the time, however, didn't agree with my excitement over my budding relationship with Joe. They both cautioned me not to get involved with him because he was on the rebound from his previous long-term relationship. But I was caught up in the all-consuming warmth and excitement of new love, and I ignored their warnings. Looking back, I'm so glad I didn't take their advice. I may have been his rebound relationship when he kissed me and asked me to be his girlfriend on July 8, 1994, but I was the center of his world when he asked me to marry him on July 8, 1997.

When he proposed, he first gave me an ID bracelet engraved with my name on the front and the date on the back. He then said, "I have something else for you, but it's not wrapped. How do you wrap a last name?" I nearly melted to the floor!

We were married in June 1998. Joe and I had a simple wedding with the ceremony in our church's sanctuary and the reception in the church hall, catered by an older couple who were also members. To me, the most important requirement for the wedding was to have a professional photographer, but I feared we would never find one that fit our small budget. When I found an affordable photographer who had been recommended by a friend, I was thrilled!

One afternoon I was discussing my plans with my mother, and my father came into the kitchen. I looked over at him and said, "Dad, you're going to walk me down the aisle, right?"

He looked surprised. "I thought I would embarrass you."

Tears filled my eyes when I imagined that tradition missing from my special day. "I would be embarrassed if you didn't walk me down the aisle."

All of our plans came together, and our wedding day was perfect! Many special people attended our wedding, including Joe's grandmother, our only living grandparent, who traveled from Illinois to celebrate with us. Other friends and family members traveled from as far away as Florida, Illinois, Texas, New Jersey, and Maine. Dad walked me down the aisle, and we were surrounded by friends and family as we took our vows and pledged our lives to each other. This was a new beginning, a new chapter in my life. I was marrying my best friend and taking on a new name.

After the ceremony and photos, we joined our guests in the church hall and celebrated with food and dancing. The wedding guests showered us with bubbles when we left the reception, and we found our Jeep Wagoneer decorated with signs declaring us "Just Married." Soon we were headed to the Outer Banks for our honeymoon.

After the wedding and honeymoon, we quickly settled into our new lives.

Due to my father's handicaps, my mother finally decided they should get a smaller, more manageable house. My parents sold their dream home and downsized to a smaller one in the same neighborhood. At the same time, Joe and I purchased a small ranch house a couple of blocks from his parents' home in a neighborhood called Rock Creek.

After we settled in, I spent an afternoon going through old home movies alone. I found a video I had shot in my brother's home when my parents and I had visited him and his family in New Jersey. In the video, my toddler nephew walked around the apartment. In the background of the video I heard a familiar voice talking nonstop about a political issue. At first I didn't recognize the voice, and then it hit me like a ton of bricks — the voice belonged to my father. It was the voice I'd grown up with. The words were clear, and his intonation was warm and comforting. It was the voice of my daddy, the man who had raised me.

My eyes filled with tears, and I sobbed uncontrollably. I'd missed that voice so much. My father's voice had changed since the stroke. Not only were his words now slurred, but the tone of his voice had changed as well.

Hearing his former voice was too much for me to handle. My heart crumbled as memories swirled through my mind — trips to Disney World, vacations in the Adirondacks, evenings spent on our little back porch in Jersey watching thunderstorms. Everything we'd lost the day of my father's stroke overcame me, and I nearly drowned in the bereavement.

Joe arrived home and found me bawling like a baby in front of the television.

"What are you doing?" he asked, confused.

"I found this video of my dad." I sniffed and wiped my eyes. "That's his voice, his *real* voice. That's how he sounded before the stroke." I pointed toward the television.

"Turn it off." His voice was gentle but also firm. "Stop torturing yourself like this."

"I wish you could've known him before the stroke," I told Joe while turning off the video. "He was brilliant and funny. He would've loved to talk cars with you."

Joe nodded and gave me a sad smile. "I can tell he's brilliant, but you need to stop hurting yourself like this. Okay?"

"Yeah." I wiped my eyes. "I will."

Although I promised Joe I would stop torturing myself, I couldn't prevent myself from wondering what life could've been like if my father had been healthy when I met Joe. Dad wasn't a mechanic by trade, but he knew enough about cars to get by. In fact, he'd tried more than once to teach me how to check the oil and change a tire on my Nissan, but I had never paid enough attention to actually learn how to do it. I could imagine my father visiting with Joe while Joe worked on one of his car projects. Maybe Dad would've even lent Joe a hand. But that could now never happen.

I broke down once again while Joe and I were having dinner at my parents' new house in Pine Meadows. I was watching my father struggle to eat with his utensils and I dissolved into tears before running into one of their spare bedrooms. Joe and my mother looked at me as if I were crazy and needed professional help. I was, however, overwhelmed with grief over my father's handicaps. I felt it wasn't fair that my father had to struggle to do simple tasks. He had once been a man who could build small furniture, such as the cedar chest my mother used to store blankets in, and the knife block in my kitchen. After the stroke he could barely carve a piece of meat, much less craft a piece of furniture.

I was baptized as a baby and raised Lutheran. Since childhood I have had a very strong faith. When I was young, I would lie in bed at night and talk to God for hours, pouring out my heart and sharing my hopes and fears. I've always believed Jesus Christ is my savior, and God hears and answers our prayers. I grew up attending church with my parents in New Jersey, and we quickly found a church when we moved to Virginia Beach. Although my father didn't attend church every week, my mother and I went nearly every Sunday.

My faith changed when my father had his stroke. I was infuriated with God, and I turned my back on him. I was angry he'd let my precious daddy have a stroke and left him a shell of the man he once was. I refused to go to church. The Sunday after my father's stroke, my mother went to church and cried to the minister. After that she faithfully continued going to church every Sunday while I stayed home. I didn't pray; in fact, I stopped talking to God altogether.

Despite Joe's and my new friends, that time without God in my life was lonely. I had no hope and I felt hollow inside. Something was missing from my life, and I soon realized I needed my faith in order to survive. I don't remember how long I was angry with God, but I eventually realized how wrong I was to blame God for my father's stroke. After all, it was Dad who had defied the doctors and stopped taking his blood pressure medicine, a decision with catastrophic consequences.

Around that time my mother began looking for a new church. My heart had softened, and I understood how wrong I was to stop going to church. I needed to fill that hole in my life. I needed God. I told her I would go with her.

We visited a new church and immediately felt at home. The congregation was affable and welcoming, and it was just what we needed during that arduous time. Walking into the sanctuary warmed my soul. When I opened my heart in prayer, my faith was renewed. My mother and I became members of the church, and I quickly became active in the congregation. I joined the altar guild, participated in the vocal and bell choirs, and taught Sunday school. Although life was still difficult at times, I felt a spark of renewal. Having God back in my life made me whole again. I was ready to sincerely focus not only on him but also on my new life with Joe.

Chapter Five

SERIOUSLY SICK

IN THE EARLY YEARS AFTER HIS stroke, my father managed to do small jobs around the house. He took care of the housecleaning, laundry, and yard. In the late 1990s, however, my father's health began declining. He did fewer tasks and spent most of his time in his recliner watching television. Joe constantly dropped by to help my parents. He would do little things and sometimes even mow their lawn. It was as if Joe had two houses to maintain.

I felt bad for Joe having to run over and help my parents all the time, and I also felt bad for my mother, who needed the help. My mother is and was my best friend and greatest confidante. So one evening I called her and decided to bring up an idea that I had been contemplating.

"I was thinking about something," I began. "I've noticed that Dad is doing less and less around the house, and Joe has been going to your place more often to help you out."

"That's true," Mom said. "Dad is having a hard time cutting the grass lately, and I can't take care of it because I'm working full-time."

"What if we found a two-family house? That way Joe and I could help you out more easily."

"How do you think Joe would feel about that?"

I shrugged. "I don't think he'd have a problem. You know how easygoing he is. It would make life a lot easier for you, and Joe wouldn't have to take care of two houses anymore."

"It sounds like a great idea, but I think you need to talk to your husband about it first."

That night I shared my idea with Joe, and he quickly said yes. We planned to sell both of our homes and find a two-family duplex or a single-family home with a downstairs master bedroom for my parents.

In the fall of 1999, we found the perfect house in a brand-new planned neighborhood called Castleton in Virginia Beach. The model home had everything we needed, so we put a contract in and then prayed both our houses would sell.

In preparation for putting our 1,046-square-foot house on the market, we entered into a whirlwind of cosmetic renovations and curb-appeal updates. Among other things, Joe painted the walls and ceiling of the attached one-car garage with a potent primer ... without wearing a mask. Later we would wonder if the fumes caused Joe's problems. At the time, though, we were blissfully unaware and focused on selling our old home and building a new one.

My parents' house sold quickly, but ours was a little trickier. Our house was small, and it had only two bedrooms, making it a less desirable home. I prayed we'd find the right person to fall in love with it, as we had when we bought it. Thankfully, someone did — the house finally sold during the holidays. I'd thought putting a tree up in the family room would make the house look smaller, but my realtor insisted it would make it seem homier. She was right; the house sold to a single woman.

Since both our house and my parents' home had sold, we had to rent while the new house was being built. It was winter and off-season for tourists, so we got a great deal on a house out at Sandbridge Beach. We rented a place called The Kiwi, a one-level clapboard house located one block from the oceanfront. Although the house may have been perfect for a summer getaway, it wasn't insulated for winter. To survive the cold nights, we had to sleep under piles of blankets!

The house had a host of other issues that would've kept a handyman busy. The roof leaked, and there were clear termite trails climbing the walls. But we took advantage of the deck on top of the roof, watching the stars and enjoying the comforting cadence of the waves. It was a time of joyful planning for our future home.

Little did we know we were about to embark on a long, scary journey that would change our lives forever.

It began one day when Joe noticed his legs were swelling. The swelling persisted for a few days. Concerned, he went to a local urgent care center, and called me after a test showed he was losing protein in his urine.

"You have protein in your urine?" I asked when he told me the news. "I'm confused. What does that mean?"

"It means there may be something wrong with my kidneys,"

Joe explained. "The doctor said I need to be referred to a kidney specialist. Do you know the name of the doctor your father sees?"

I told him the name. "Are they going to make an appointment for you?" I asked.

"Yes," Joe said. "They'll make the referral."

At that time, I thought it wasn't a big deal; Joe rarely visited the doctor or complained of not feeling well. He'd been healthy all his life. So I was certain he'd take a few medications and then all would return to normal.

Unfortunately, that was not the case. Joe was seriously sick, and his illness was fast moving. The clinical term for his condition was *membranous glomerulopathy*, meaning the filters were damaged in both of his kidneys, preventing them from cleaning toxins out of the blood properly. So he was literally being poisoned by his own body.

His kidney disease wasn't hereditary, nor genetic. The best guess the doctors could give us was that Joe had come into contact with a chemical that had caused the damage. The damage, he explained, could have happened earlier in Joe's life while he worked on cars, or it could have been something else. The doctors said there was no way of knowing. My own personal theory was the primer he used to paint our tiny garage in Virginia Beach, since the swelling in his legs occurred just two months after he painted.

But in the end, did the cause of the disease really matter? We didn't have time to focus on the what-ifs and the hows. We were beginning a life-and-death battle.

Once the diagnosis was made, Joe quickly went to see the

nephrologist, the same one my father was seeing. The doctor soon called a family meeting. Joe's parents, his brother, his brother's girlfriend, and I gathered with Joe and the doctor in the waiting area of the office to discuss the road ahead for Joe. My stomach clenched and I held my breath while the doctor talked about dialysis and a possible kidney transplant. It was surreal to hear these serious and terrifying medical terms used in a conversation about my husband. How was it possible that my formerly healthy husband was facing dialysis and needing a kidney transplant? After the meeting, Jason, Joe's younger brother, touched Joe's arm and said, "Hey, man, if you need a kidney, I'll give you one."

My heart warmed at the words, and the simple statement gave me hope. Even though we were facing this huge, scary, uncertain future, I believed the Lord would get us through it. Somehow.

In fact, he gave us something to help keep our minds off things. On Memorial Day weekend of 2000 — the same weekend we closed on our new house — we found out I was pregnant. Talk about a seesaw of emotion — we zoomed from lows to highs! I was elated! I'd dreamt of starting a family when we moved into our new home, and the dream had come one step closer to reality. I couldn't wait to make plans for the baby.

I wanted to be surprised about the sex of the baby, but Joe insisted we find out what we were having so that we could plan. We were excited to find out that our baby was going to be a boy. Since Joe is actually Joseph Martin Clipston III, I told him we could name the baby Joseph Martin IV, as long as we called him "Joey" and not "Marty." (Joe's family calls him Marty, but it sounds foreign to me. I was introduced to him as Joe, so he'll always be Joe to me.)

Joe disagreed. He said the name stopped with him. He called up his mother and said, "It's a boy. It's not going to be Joseph Martin IV. You can just get over it." I was stunned he was so outspoken with his mother, but I respected his decision.

Still, we needed a name. "Do you like the name Matthew?" I asked him one day while we were watching television in the room over the garage. "It's my top choice. We can call him Matt. I like names with built-in nicknames since I never had one."

"Nah." Joe shook his head.

"How about Aidan?" I suggested. "That's a really unusual name."

"Aidan?" He scrunched his nose as if he smelled something disgusting. "No way. I always liked the name Lance."

"Lance?" I regarded the name with disgust. "I don't think so. That sounds like a surfer dude. Do you like the names Cody or Dylan?"

"No." He shook his head.

"Hmm." I glanced down at the list of names I had scribbled in a notebook. "I always thought Zac was a cool name. Do you like Zachary?"

"Zachary Clipston." Joe rubbed his chin. "Yeah, that sounds good."

And there you have it. Zachary was only one of the names on my list, but it was the only one we could agree on. We're lucky we didn't have a girl because we couldn't agree on any girl's names. The poor baby would've been unnamed for days had she been a girl, which is what happened when I was born.

My father seriously wanted the name Max, even when he found out I was a girl. He was convinced that Max Goebelbecker was a fabulous name. My mother refused, and I was unnamed for three days until my mother insisted they name me Amy. Thank goodness she won that argument!

Chapter Six

New Beginnings

By this point we'd finally moved into our dream home. Joe and I made an extra room into an office, where I set up a computer desk and began writing fiction late into the night. My parents quickly settled into the house as well, and my father enjoyed watching television in his new family room as if he'd lived there for years.

I'd always thought I'd decorate my first baby's room in a Disney theme, since I'd been a Disney fanatic for years and had managed to acquire quite a few collectibles and framed artwork. I changed my mind when we found out we were going to have a boy. Instead, I suggested we decorate the baby's room in a NASCAR theme. Joe was thrilled — and it was a great way to keep his mind off his kidney issues. At that time, NASCAR wasn't quite as popular as it is now, and it was more difficult to find collectibles. Joe happily spent hours scouring stores for decorations. He found a wallpaper border and signs. Meanwhile I found posters and had them framed. It was the cutest room!

Zachary was due on Super Bowl Sunday, which was January 28, 2001. Everyone told me first babies are always late, but Zac had other plans. My water broke on January 21 while we were getting ready for church. I was stunned! I'd never imagined my first baby would come a week early. I tried my best not to panic as I told my mother and Joe that it was time to go. My mother didn't believe me. She thought I was making it up since her water didn't break on its own when she had my brother or me. I remember telling her I wasn't lying and I wasn't wetting my pants — my water had broken!

I was petrified. The day I had been dreaming of since the previous May had finally come. I was going to become a mother! Panic and excitement surged through me at the thought of meeting my baby boy for the first time. It was time to go!

I could say Zac's birth was all sweet and lovely, but I'd be lying. Zachary's delivery was excruciating. I was in labor for thirty-six hours and pushed for a total of five hours.

At one point, my obstetrician came to check on me. After a brief exam she frowned at me. "I'll give you one more hour of pushing. If that doesn't work, then you're going to have to have a cesarean."

I stupidly took that as a threat and yelled, "No!"

That was the worst decision I could've made. When Zachary Taylor Clipston was finally born, a neonatal pediatrician was waiting for him. I had only a second to give my newborn baby a kiss on his little nose before he was immediately whisked off to the neonatal intensive care unit. Apparently Zachary's birth was so rough on his little body that he blew a hole in his lung, making breathing difficult. He spent the first four days of his life in the NICU with a chest tube.

Meanwhile I felt as if I'd been run over by a steamroller. My whole body ached, and I couldn't stand without assistance. The first night in the hospital was difficult. I couldn't sleep, and I couldn't stop worrying about Zachary. I stared at the television for hours. A nurse finally took pity on me, put me in a wheelchair, and pushed me over to the NICU, where I was able to reach out and touch Zachary's little arm. I wanted to hold him close and study every detail of his little face, but I wasn't permitted to take him out of his small bassinet. It was agony to look at him but not be allowed to hold him.

The hospital released me the next day, and I felt empty coming home without my baby boy. But we visited him every day, and eventually I was allowed to hold him. I spent hours snuggling him and feeding him with a little bottle. At first I felt sorry for myself for having to visit my newborn in the NICU, but my perspective changed when I spotted tiny premature twins who had been in the hospital for more than a month. I knew then I was blessed to only have to wait a few days for my baby to come home.

We were overwhelmed with joy on the day they finally released Zac to us. We loaded him in the car and brought him home for lots of photo ops. My dream of a family — in our new home — was realized at last.

Chapter Seven

DAD'S SLOW DECLINE

LIFE SETTLED INTO A ROUTINE. TAKING care of Zac, taking care of Joe, helping Mom take care of Dad. As Zac passed milestone after milestone — first tooth, first word, first time crawling — Joe and I tried to focus on the good in our lives. But life with my father in the house was proving more difficult than we'd imagined. As his health declined, he became more and more depressed and cantankerous. He had little patience with Zac as he began to toddle around and make noise. I had a difficult time holding back my temper when my father would fuss at him for being too loud while he was trying to listen to the television through his headphones. Our big, beautiful house began to feel too small.

One day I returned home from work and found my mother making supper.

"How was your day?" she asked while stirring a pot full of spaghetti.

"Fine. How was yours?" I dropped my bag next to a chair.

"Well, your father yelled at Zac again while he was playing near the television set." She glowered. "I'm getting tired of reminding him that Zac is only a baby. I think we need to do something about it."

"What do you mean?" I leaned against the counter.

"I think it would help if we added on a playroom." She pointed toward the French doors leading to our small deck. "We could take the deck down and add on a little sunroom."

I grimaced. "I don't know. That would be pretty expensive."

"But it sure would eliminate a lot of my stress." She stirred the spaghetti again. "We could put all of Zac's toys in there, along with a television. If Zac had his own space, he could play without interfering with your dad's television shows. I would be nearby if your dad needed me, and Zac would have his own space."

"Okay. Let's look into it."

After taking out a loan, we added a small room with large windows and a sliding glass door that led out to a small patio. Now Zac had a place to play without bothering my father.

But irritability wasn't the only issue with my father. His health issues and physical disabilities became more stressful as time went on, until the day the unthinkable happened — Dad tried to commit suicide. In a fit of rage, he deliberately took too much insulin, and we had to call 911. I couldn't believe how changed my father was from the man he'd been. And I felt so guilty for being angry with him. Here I was supposed to be loving and supporting him, and all I could think about was how difficult he'd become to live with. And poor Joe ... I'm convinced there's a special place in heaven for Joe because he willingly agreed to live with my parents and endure all of the stress.

We were grateful that my father didn't take enough insulin to do any damage, and he didn't need to be examined by a doctor. Not only was I worried about my father's health after the incident, I was also concerned about my mother's stress level. His attempted suicide was difficult for her to handle, but I was glad Joe and I were there to support her.

Chapter Eight

DOCTOR ROULETTE

As we learned how to compromise in our family household and experienced the joys of parenthood, Joe's illness became an ever-present cloud over our heads. I can't describe the helplessness I felt in those days. My personality is geared toward *doing*, but there was nothing I could do. I wanted to fix the situation; I wanted to fix Joe. But I didn't know how or what to do.

Compounding my anxiety, Joe's doctor delayed making a referral to the Sentara Norfolk General Transplant Center to start the process toward a kidney transplant. Although we'd sat with his doctor and discussed dialysis and transplant options, a year later we still had no game plan for Joe. It was as if we were sitting with our hands in our pockets feeling helpless while Joe steadily lost kidney function. I have since met kidney patients who avoided dialysis and had a transplant without becoming as ill as Joe was. Looking back, I'm frustrated by what Joe had to endure during that time, but we simply didn't know there was any other alternative.

I became more and more frustrated. To be honest, Joe and I had several disagreements about finding a new kidney specialist. I felt deep in my heart that another doctor would be more proactive with Joe's illness as his kidney function continued to plummet. I had no control over the dreadful disease or its progression, but I could at least help Joe find a better healthcare provider.

One day a coworker recommended a nephrologist who had helped her husband through a successful transplant. Could this be what we needed? I was determined to convince Joe to meet with the specialist and get a second opinion. Later that evening, I broached the subject while we were getting ready for bed.

"My coworker told me that she loves her husband's nephrologist," I said as I climbed into bed. "Her husband had a successful kidney transplant a few years ago. She said his doctor is really wonderful. He's easy to talk to and very knowledgeable."

"That's good." Joe sat on the edge of the bed.

"I think you should talk to his doctor just to get another opinion. It never hurts to talk to someone else, especially when it comes to your health."

"Where is his office?"

"It's right near where I work, in the medical tower by the hospital. I can call and make an appointment." I held my breath and prayed that Joe would agree to it.

He shrugged. "Okay."

The doctor's office was located in Norfolk near the hospital.

Joe and I went together, and I immediately liked the doctor, who was affable and amusing. He welcomed us into his office with a big smile, and he refused to charge us for the visit because, as he declared, "Information is free." I liked the sound of that!

The doctor listened to Joe's story. He agreed Joe's illness may have been caused by contact with chemicals, whether while working on cars or painting the garage. He told us about a patient of his who had worked in construction. The man used a chemical on a Friday and the following week wound up in the doctor's office with protein in his urine, just like Joe had.

Joe and I both liked this doctor. I felt comfortable with him, and I had a feeling he would take good care of Joe. Although he didn't offer us any more insight into Joe's care, the doctor's bedside manner and genuine smile gave me something the first doctor hadn't — hope. I wanted Joe to start seeing him right away . . . but Joe refused! He remained faithful to his first doctor. I was frustrated, but I didn't give up. I was convinced I would find better care for Joe, no matter what it took.

So I kept looking. Another friend told me about Duke University and how they had one of the best kidney programs in the country. Out of pure desperation, I emailed the kidney team at Duke University and shared Joe's story. The team at Duke immediately answered and said Joe's case was urgent since he was so young. The contact there agreed to see us and gave us an appointment for the following week. I again felt a glimmer of hope that this hospital could give us some answers and also help slow the progression of Joe's disease. Despite Joe's hesitation, I insisted we visit them for another opinion.

Joe and I both took a day off work and drove to Raleigh,

North Carolina, to meet with the Duke University kidney team. Another couple — close family friends — traveled with us, and we visited a few NASCAR race shops on the way. Experiencing the race shops was a nice distraction from the reality of Joe's failing health. While we shopped for our favorite memorabilia and gasped at real-life racecars that had been driven by Dale Earnhardt and Dale Earnhardt Jr., I pretended my life was normal and my husband didn't have a serious chronic illness. Instead of being a caregiver, I was just another NASCAR fan and tourist enjoying a day at the race shop.

But it was impossible to hide very long from our reality. Throughout the trip Joe was exhausted, and he spent most of the time sleeping in the car. As his kidney function slipped, he was losing more and more of his energy. I prayed our trip to Duke would bring some miraculous solution to his condition. Perhaps these experts held the key to making my husband healthy again!

When we arrived at Duke, our friends waited in the car while Joe and I entered the medical facility. I immediately felt my mood change from the happy excitement I'd felt at the race shops. The dark cloud of Joe's illness covered us like a suffocating blanket. I fidgeted and worried while we sat in the waiting room. When we moved to the exam room, we met with two young doctors who had reviewed Joe's case. Unfortunately, the doctors held no secret miracle drug for Joe. They didn't tell us anything different from what we'd heard from the other doctors we'd visited.

I pondered all this during the long ride back to Virginia Beach. Once Joe and I were alone in our bedroom at home, I decided to lay my feelings out on the line and beg him to change doctors. I wanted him to start seeing my coworker's doctor, who had been so pleasant and personable. And I was so sure I could convince Joe to see the situation my way.

But things didn't go as planned. Despite the two second opinions, Joe still held a blind faith in his doctor. He refused to leave this man, no matter what I did. I tried reasoning with him calmly, but nothing I said seemed to work. Soon we were screaming at each other, and I was crying infuriated and exasperated tears. Why didn't Joe understand I had only his best interest in mind? Couldn't he see I wanted him healthy and I was certain his doctor wasn't doing all he could to make Joe better?

Out of desperation, I tried appealing to his parents, hoping Joe's father could convince him to leave the nephrologist. To my surprise, Joe's parents also liked this doctor. In fact, his father had talked to friends in the medical community who endorsed this doctor. Without his parents' support, I was rendered defenseless in my argument. It was as if no one would listen to me, and I was screaming my frustrations at a brick wall. I was discouraged and exhausted. All of my pleading and begging with Joe had been in vain.

Joe and I eventually moved past our argument, and I swallowed my resentment toward the doctor. Yet in my heart, I believed Joe could get better care if he would only go to another medical group.

Chapter Nine

THE DIALYSIS DECISION

IN EARLY MARCH OF 2003, JOE called me at work after leaving a routine appointment with his nephrologist.

"My numbers are really bad. I have to start dialysis." As he spoke, his voice cracked, echoing my own despair, and the sound of his anguish was too much for me to handle.

"When?" I asked as tears filled my eyes.

"Soon. Like in a week or so."

"We'll get through it," I promised, despite my own quavering voice.

I tried to hold it together while he shared the doctor's plan for what would come next, but soon we were both sobbing. It was a surreal nightmare. I was certain our world was falling apart. Joe's kidney disease had progressed quickly, and the abstract concept of dialysis was now a reality for us. I had never imagined Joe and I would face an illness together, especially during the early years of our marriage. While most newlyweds dealt with the simple adjustments of learning how to live with someone, our relationship was being forged in the fire of illness. We couldn't run and hide from it. We needed to face it head-on, and I wasn't sure I was strong enough. I felt my life spiraling out of control, but I kept my fears to myself while I spoke to Joe. I couldn't burden him with my fears when he was already trying to sort through his own.

We'd studied the basics of dialysis, but now we had to become experts. Dialysis is the artificial process of ridding the blood of waste and unwanted water, and is required when the process can't be completed by the kidneys. There are two methods: peritoneal and hemodialysis. My coworker helped us sort through the issues to decide which type to choose.

With the peritoneal method, the patient dialyzes himself four times per day with the aid of bags of saline. The process uses the patient's peritoneum in the abdomen as a membrane across which fluids and dissolved substances are exchanged from the blood. Fluid is introduced through a permanent tube in the abdomen and flushed out via regular exchanges throughout the day, a process which takes forty-five minutes apiece. Peritoneal dialysis is significantly less costly, with the primary advantage being the ability to treat yourself without visiting a medical facility. The main complication of peritoneal dialysis is infection at the site of the permanent tube in the abdomen.

The hemodialysis method takes place in a dialysis center. Three times a week, the patient is hooked up to a dialysis machine for approximately four hours. The patient has the benefit of medical care during the process, but my coworker explained that with this method there are highs and lows. When a patient leaves the hemodialysis treatment, he feels the high of having all of the toxins cleaned out of his body. But that doesn't last. By the time the patient goes back for a treatment two days later, he has reached a low due to the buildup of toxins in the body. This contrasts with the daily cleansing of the peritoneal method.

At my coworker's recommendation, Joe chose the peritoneal method. He knew he would have more energy and feel better by performing the peritoneal method since he would dialyze more often than with the hemodialysis method.

My coworker told us her husband felt so well on peritoneal dialysis that he built a shed in the backyard in the dead of winter by himself! That was incredible news to us; we never imagined a dialysis patient could have that much ambition and energy. Since Joe's favorite pastime was working on cars, and he worked as an auto body technician, the story gave us both hope that he could live a normal life while enduring daily dialysis treatments.

Joe had a port surgically inserted into his abdomen, and he then performed his exchanges four times each day while working full-time at the auto body repair shop.

I could count on the phone ringing around 4 p.m. every day while I was at work.

"Hello?" I said one afternoon, answering the phone at my desk.

"Hey." Joe's voice rang through the receiver. "What's up?"

"Nothing." I wound the cord around my finger while I talked. "I guess you're doing your exchange."

"Yup." He sighed. "Just sitting in the break room watching Oprah."

"Oprah, huh?" I grinned. "I guess nothing else is on."

"Nope. We don't have cable, so I don't have much choice."

I laughed, thinking how funny it sounded for him to discuss the talk show with me while he sat in a shop filled with male workers.

I was thankful for the humorous Oprah conversations, which seemed to lighten our distress about his health. My goal was to learn how to laugh and stay positive despite his chronic illness.

At home, our son Zac, who was two years old by this time, sat with Joe during treatments. Of course, Zac had no idea his daddy was ill. I often wondered if he thought everyone's daddy had to give himself treatments with bags of fluid with the assistance of an IV pole. Zac doesn't remember those times now, but he seemed to enjoy that special time with Daddy. Seeing them together warmed my heart and made me smile.

All of Joe's treatments, however, weren't happy times filled with father-son bonding and discussions revolving around Oprah guests. In fact, dialysis is akin to a prison sentence for patients. Joe had constant stomach issues and was so ill some days that he stayed in his recliner. Traveling was often a hassle, since Joe would have to pack his dialysis supplies along with the pharmacy of medications he had to ingest daily to keep his blood pressure, calcium, phosphorus, and anemia regulated.

In fact, we had to clean out an entire closet for his dialysis supplies. A truck would come monthly with nearly a hundred boxes of the bags of solution. We soon became accustomed to the routine of the truck coming and of filling up the closet. It was a normal part of our lives to discuss when the next dialysis delivery would arrive. It's funny how we learn to adapt to such grievous situations. Ironically, I grew to like the leftover supply boxes since they were sturdy and convenient for packing things up for the attic.

Chapter Ten

AN UNEXPECTED LOSS

WHEN JOE FIRST WENT ON DIALYSIS, I was pregnant with our second child. This pregnancy was a silver lining in Joe's illness, a promise God would continue to bless us despite the ever-present dark cloud of chronic illness. This child was also an answer to one of my most fervent prayers: that I would have two children. I longed to give Zachary a sibling, someone who would be a part of his life after Joe and I were gone. Our unborn child also assured us that life would be normal and wonderful again someday. I held this pregnancy close to my heart and put all of my hope in it.

Unlike my first pregnancy, however, I suffered complications in the first trimester. During the first week Joe started dialysis, I traveled to New Jersey to be an attendant in my childhood best friend Christine's wedding. I was concerned about leaving Zachary since Joe was coping with his first week of dialysis, but Joe's mother was on hand to look out for both Joe and Zac.

I realized I was spotting blood when my mother and I first arrived in New Jersey. Mom and I were shopping at a Kohl's near my aunt's house when I found the blood. I immediately panicked, and with my heart pounding in my chest, I frantically called my obstetrician's office from the shopping mall parking lot. They recommended I go straight to an emergency room. My mother and I met up with my aunt and then headed to the nearest hospital. During the short ride to the hospital I prayed, begging God to take care of my baby. I couldn't imagine losing the child — the embodiment of all my hopes and dreams for a happy future. When we arrived at the hospital, I rushed in and begged the receptionist to help me right away.

Despite my urgency, we spent that entire evening waiting around at Valley Hospital, in Ridgewood, which, ironically, was where I was born. The ultrasound technician was leaving when I arrived, and no one stopped her to tell her she had a patient waiting. The hospital finally called her and she came back.

I held my breath while the technician administered an ultra-sound to check my growing baby. I prayed continuously while I stared at the screen, waiting to hear her conclusion. When she told us the fetus was still developing, we all breathed a deep sigh of relief. We thought everything was going to be okay, and I felt my body relax. My mother and I were able to attend the wedding, and I was excited to be able to celebrate Christine's happy day with her.

Unfortunately, the spotting persisted and eventually trans-formed into bleeding. My hope for the baby slowly deflated like a balloon. Although a few more ultrasounds showed the fetus was developing correctly, a feeling of dread pooled in my stomach and lingered. Some days I was positive we were going to welcome this new child into our family, and other days I was certain that the pregnancy was going to come to an end. But even on the best of days, I believed deep in my heart that something was wrong with the fetus. I was scared both of losing the child and losing all that this child represented for me, my family, and our future.

When the bleeding increased, I told my mother I was tired of the roller coaster of emotions. "If I'm going to lose this baby, I want to just get it over with, mourn, and move on," I said to my mother. "I can't live this way anymore. It's too much to bear."

Twenty-four hours later, the pain and bleeding intensified. I called the obstetrician's office, and the doctor on call said, "It's either the beginning of something or the end of something. Take some Advil and go to bed." When I asked if the Advil would hurt the baby, the doctor said, "At this point, that doesn't matter."

The pain increased to nearly intolerable levels in the middle of the night. I got up, went to the bathroom, and found I was miscarrying. The pressure and cramps were excruciating. I was terrified, and I didn't want to be alone. I yelled out to Joe, and he jumped out of bed. I told him what was happening, and he stared at me helplessly.

"I need my mom," I said, holding onto the sink. "Please go get her."

He looked at the clock and hesitated. "But it's three in the morning," he said.

"I don't care!" I yelled. "I need my mother *now!*"

"Okay." He hurried downstairs.

At that moment, I knew he could never understand what I was going through. I realized it was the middle of the night. But my mom was the only one who could comfort me at this moment, and I knew she would want to be there to hold my hand. Only she would understand since she had experienced the agonizing loss of multiple miscarriages.

My mother came, and we both cried. We knew the roller coaster ride had finally ended. I had lost the baby at sixteen weeks. Although I was distraught over the loss, I also had an overwhelming sense of relief. I could now concentrate on taking care of Joe and being the best mother I could to Zac.

The following day I went to see my obstetrician. The delay in the waiting room was torturous. I sat surrounded by happy pregnant women who were rubbing their big bellies and sharing ultrasound photos. I couldn't help but envy their healthy pregnancies and imagined their lives were perfect and free from the stress I endured every day. I knew it was immature and petty to look at strangers and envy them, but I couldn't help it. I wallowed in self-pity.

I was taken into an exam room, and the nurse practitioner performed an ultrasound, showing no trace of the fetus was left. Everything was gone, the pregnancy over. I felt empty. All of the plans I'd made for the child were gone literally overnight. The names I'd played around with in my head and written with a flourish in a notebook were invalid. The mental designs for the nursery dissolved. My hopes and dreams of a larger family disappeared in a flash. I couldn't hold back my tears, and the nurse practitioner held my hand and cried along with my mother and me.

The nurse practitioner asked me why I hadn't gone to the emergency room after the miscarriage, and I explained to her that the doctor on call had told me to take Advil and go to bed. She was stunned. She told me I should have gone to the emergency room because I could have bled to death. This news shocked me. I had never imagined I could die from a miscarriage. I was thankful to be okay despite the poor advice of the doctor on call the night before.

When my mother and I left my doctor's office, I called Joe from the car while my mom drove.

"Hi," I said when he answered.

"What did the doctor say?" Joe's voice was hopeful.

"It's gone." My voice quavered with the bereavement I'd been trying to suppress after talking to the nurse practitioner. "It's all gone. There was nothing on the ultrasound."

I heard Joe heave a breath and then begin to sob into the phone. My heart broke once again because Joe had held onto hope that the baby would be okay. I'd had the suspicion the night before that the pregnancy was over. Hearing him cry made me realize Joe still had to go through all of the steps of grief I had already moved through in my mind. While he was still mourning the child, I had an overwhelming sense of peace and relief after worrying and praying for weeks. Now that it was over, I could move past the anxiety and accept it wasn't God's plan for us to have another baby at that time.

I took a week off of work and asked my closest coworkers not to send out any news about my miscarriage. I didn't want to be the object of their pity, and I wanted to keep the miscarriage confidential. Nevertheless, some colleagues found out, and I had to endure ignorant comments such as, "God needed another angel" or "It just wasn't the right time for you to have a baby." Although I was devastated over losing the baby, I tried my best to ignore the misguided words and just focus on all of my blessings.

I focused on what was important — I celebrated Zac and had his portrait taken wearing a bright yellow SpongeBob T-shirt. Although my hope was that Joe and I would have another child in order to give Zac a sibling, I was happy that despite Joe's illness we had one healthy child. I was blessed many times over with my family, despite our challenges with Joe's illness.

After my miscarriage, my dear friend Michele gave me a beautiful angel pin — the very same pin I wore the day I was hit by the semi in 2008. The pin is very special to me because it reminds me of the baby I lost, but it also reminds me of the special friends I had in Virginia. I will always treasure my special pin and my friendship with Michele.

Chapter Eleven

GIVE AND TAKE

JOE AND I CLICKED THE FIRST TIME WE MET. It was as if we had a special connection and we "got" each other. We always tease each other and tend to be very sarcastic. I can always count on Joe to give me a hard time, especially if I say something silly or make a mistake. I know it's all in fun, and I look forward to his smart comments. I've learned, however, that not every couple behaves like we do.

Once while spending time with one of my friends, Joe and I were giving each other a hard time. When Joe walked away, my friend said, "Do you and Joe like each other?"

I laughed and said, "Of course we do. Why do you ask?"

She shook her head. "I could never talk to my husband that way."

I couldn't help but think it was a shame that she felt that way. If you can't tease your spouse, then who can you tease?

Our relationship isn't based only on smart comments and teasing, however. We also have a loving side. Joe and I hold hands in the car and also in the movie theater. He ends every phone call by saying "I love you" before he hangs up, and he sends cute text messages frequently during the day. He randomly hugs me, pokes me, or rubs my back whenever I pass by him in the house. Aside from my mother, he's my biggest supporter when it comes to my writing.

He's also a wonderful listener. If I've had a bad day at work, I can count on him to listen to my rant and take my side when I complain about the job stress. I've always known I could count on Joe, no matter what. I could never relate to coworkers who complained about their spouses because I can honestly say that Joe is my best friend.

Our relationship changed drastically, however, when Joe went on dialysis. The warm, funny man I'd known since my senior year in college suddenly changed. He turned moody, and his health was unpredictable. Our days of going out to dinner and spending quiet time together suddenly evaporated. Our relationship had taken a new turn, and I didn't know how to handle it.

One evening I found him in the room over the garage lounging in his recliner while watching television. I could tell just by the expression on his face that he wasn't feeling well. And that meant our plans to go out on a date were defunct.

I flopped onto the couch and frowned. "I guess we're not going."

"My stomach is killing me." He rested his chin on his hand. "I tried taking some medicine, but it's not settling down. We'll have to try for another night."

I shook my head. This wasn't the first time, and I knew it wouldn't be the last as long as he was on dialysis. I was tired of his illness. I longed for all we'd had before he became ill. I wanted our special couple time. I craved the laughter, the teasing, and the intimacy. All I wanted was dinner out alone with Joe, but he was too ill to go. Our plans were ruined yet again by his illness.

I sighed loudly.

"You know I can't help it." I could hear his frustration.

"Yes, I do know." I stood and crossed the room before stopping in the doorway and turning to him. "But where does that leave me?"

He faced me. "What do you mean?"

"Where does this leave me?" I gestured widely. "We were supposed to go out tonight, and I was looking forward to it. We haven't spent any time together in weeks."

"I told you that I'm sick." He enunciated the words. "I can't help it. I'm sorry."

All of my frustration boiled over and I couldn't stop angry words from bursting from my lips. "We never spend any time together, and you never talk to me anymore. You just sit in the recliner and stare at the television as if I'm not there."

"It's not deliberate. You know that I wish I didn't have to deal with this. I can't help that I don't feel well."

"I know that. Believe me, it's obvious." Seething, I stomped to our room and got ready for bed.

Once in bed, I stared at the ceiling and continued my mental rant about how unfair Joe's illness was. But soon guilt crept into my soul and I regretted what I'd said to him. I knew it wasn't his fault that he didn't feel well. I was being selfish by pining over going out to dinner when he was struggling with the side effects of dialysis. I had no right to take my frustrations out on him. I knew I didn't resent him; I resented his illness. I had to apologize and let him know that I didn't blame him.

Yet I was too stubborn and prideful to go over to the room above the garage and apologize.

After what felt like hours, I heard Joe's footsteps approaching the bedroom. The bed shifted as he climbed in next to me.

"I'm sorry," I said softly.

"I am too," he said. "I know you wanted to go out tonight."

"I miss us." My voice was thick with emotion.

"I know. I miss you too. I hate that I'm sick all the time."

"I'll try to be more patient with you," I said. "But you need to try too. You need to try to talk to me more."

"Okay." He rubbed my back. "Love you."

"Love you too."

Although we faced some difficult times during Joe's kidney failure and dialysis, we made it through due to our faith in God and our faith in one another. We had seen some friends break up relationships and even divorce over petty issues, but Joe and I made it through a serious health issue and emerged stronger as a couple. We worked hard at our relationship and kept the communication open between us. And we knew what was most important in life because of what we'd been through.

Unfortunately, during this time our relationship was also tested in another way. Dad tried to take his own life again within six months of the first attempt. The second time he managed to take enough insulin to do major damage to himself. My mom and I came home from church and found him unresponsive in bed. Panicked, we called the rescue squad, and he was transported to Virginia Beach General Hospital.

My father was out of his mind, and it was harrowing for my mother and me. He spent approximately a week at the hospital. He was so agitated and aggressive that he needed round-the-clock surveillance. His doctor had a friend at the geriatric psychiatric ward in Sentara Norfolk General Hospital and was able to have my father transported there. Dad spent approximately a month at the geriatric psychiatric ward, attending counseling sessions.

My mother and I had been visiting Saint Michael Lutheran Church and immediately felt at home with the pastor and the congregation. Although the pastor had never met my father, he drove the thirty minutes from Virginia Beach to Norfolk and visited my father every day that he was in the geriatric psychiatric ward. After the first time, Pastor John called my mother and told her not to visit for a few days because my father was belligerent and abrasive. He said Dad was cursing at everyone, and he didn't want my mother to have to deal with that stress.

We were so thankful for Pastor John and his thoughtfulness during this difficult time. He gave us the comfort and strength we needed while dealing with my father's depression. He was one of the angels God put in our lives. We're so grateful we found Saint Michael Lutheran Church. The congregation was also very generous to us later, during Joe's first transplant. God led us to a wonderful congregation when we needed it most.

Although life was never perfect again with my father, things did get better. While he was still in the hospital, we had a group family counseling session. It was hurtful when my father said his outbursts were entirely my fault because I wasn't patient with him. I was impressed, however, when the counselor told my father he had to work on his anger issues and not take his frustrations with himself out on the rest of the family. The counselor gave me hope we could work through the stress of my father's illness and find a way to live together in peace.

A few days after the family counseling session, Dad checked himself out of the ward. He told the nurses he wanted to go home, and they had no legal means to keep him there for more treatment even though he needed it. I worried that his coming home early would cause things to get bad again. My mother and I wanted him to stay longer and get more help, but we couldn't make him stay. Thankfully, although the situation remained difficult, Dad never again tried to commit suicide. I'm glad he didn't put our family through that again.

Some days I wondered if our marriage could withstand the stress of both Joe's and my father's poor health. Soon, getting to the transplant center became our chief focus. The hope for a kidney transplant was the light at the end of the cold, dark, depressing tunnel of illness.

Chapter Twelve

A Brother's
Best Gift

So now we were on the transplant train, waiting and hoping. When I think back to that time, it amazes me how innocent we were. But then, it was all new and a mix of frightening and exhilarating.

Joe's mother, brother, and I were tested as possible donors. Although his mother was his best match, she was in an accident that caused her blood pressure to become elevated and made it unsafe for her to donate a kidney. The transplant coordinator told us my kidney was a good match, but Joe's brother was a better option. In the end, Joe's brother, Jason, was chosen as his donor.

We were happy about the possibility of a transplant, but it felt like a hurry-up-and-wait situation. The months dragged until a date was finally set. Since I'm impatient by nature, this was torture for me! I wanted my husband well, and I wanted him well *immediately*.

During this frustrating time, we were comforted by the outpouring of love from many family members and friends. I call these people angels, and they are a true testament of God's unfailing love. Joe's coworkers at the body shop collected money and offered emotional support. The owner of the car dealership attached to the body shop donated a large sum of money. Our church family at Saint Michael Lutheran held a silent auction and rummage sale fundraiser to assist with medical bills. A marketing and design firm donated a billboard advertising the fundraiser, and hundreds of people came. It was overwhelming to see all of the people who cared about us and wanted to help. We were very touched by their love and support during this difficult time.

Friends and family members kept Joe on prayer lists across the country. I was so grateful for everyone who remembered us and asked God to be with us. Although there were times when I would plummet into a dark abyss of worry, friends would lift me up through their encouraging words. Praying and going to church also were great sources of strength. I talked to God often, begging him to heal Joe and keep Jason safe through the transplant. Through it all, I learned who my true friends were and how much they loved my family and me.

After what seemed like a lifetime of delays, on March 29, 2004, a year after he first began peritoneal dialysis, Joe received a kidney from his brother, Jason, at Sentara Norfolk General Hospital in Norfolk, Virginia. The waiting room was packed with well-wishers the day of the transplant. Friends from my work, Joe's work, and our church waited with family members and me. The surgery seemed to last for days instead of hours. I was jittery and had a difficult time sitting still. My mind swam with worry for both Joe and Jason. I was thankful to have my pastor and friends with me to offer their support and encouraging words while we waited for news on the surgery. I prayed with friends and also kept in touch with my mother, who was at home with Zac.

Once the surgery was over, I visited Joe in recovery. As the transplant coordinator had warned me, Joe was unconscious, breathing heavily through a mask, and hooked up to several machines. The sight of my husband in such a state was jarring, even frightening. Joe's family and close friends had gone into Jason's room, leaving me to stand alone and cry in Joe's room. Although they may have been trying to give me space with my husband, I wished someone had accompanied me to Joe's room instead of filing into Jason's. I felt isolated. I needed someone there to hold my hand and tell me everything was going to be okay.

Despite all of the anxiety and frustration, the transplant initially was a success.

"Hi," I said to Joe when he finally awoke from the anesthetic. "How are you doing?"

"I'm not sure." His voice was hoarse. "How did it go?"

"It went perfectly. You look great." I touched his cheek. "Your skin is pink now. It's not yellow anymore."

"That's good."

"Yes, it is. The kidney is working." I squeezed his hand as my eyes filled with tears. "It's a miracle."

"How's Jason?" Joe's voice was still scratchy.

"He's fine. Your parents went to see him. He's doing well

too." I held onto his hand and silently thanked God for the successful transplant.

The kidney immediately began producing urine. It seemed Joe was well on the way to a great recovery. He looked healthy, which filled me with a sense of relief and hope that life would return to normal. After more than a year of declining health, he was finally getting better. I was so appreciative of the team of surgeons, and I was grateful to Jason, who had sacrificed his kidney for his brother.

Unfortunately, the first transplant had complications. One of the nurses noticed that the incision area appeared to be infected, and Joe was diagnosed with a staph infection, which delayed his release. A new team of doctors — infectious disease experts — joined the parade of medical professionals who visited him daily. At the time, I didn't realize how serious this infection was. Someone explained to me later that it could've killed him.

The days Joe spent in the hospital were exhausting for me. I visited him during my lunchtime since my office was located nearby, and I spent hours with him during the weekend. I was relieved Joe's mother would visit him at night, so that he had company and I could go home. Yet I was constantly torn between being with Joe and being home with Zac, and no matter whom I chose, I felt guilt for not being with the other instead. I felt as if I were running in circles, working and taking care of everyone except for myself. At times I wished I could clone myself and visit both places at once in order to make everyone happy. I prayed Joe would be permitted to come home soon so that I could get back to a regular routine. I craved a normal life of going to work, being home on weeknights, and enjoying my weekends.

The long fifteen days of Joe's hospital stay were particularly tiring for my mother, who was caring for our son as well as my handicapped father. I was thankful for Joe's aunt Pam, who came all the way from central Illinois to help us through the surgery. She assisted my mother with meals and caring for Zac. Pam was another angel who blessed us during that exhausting time.

Due to the staph infection, Joe had to undergo a painful surgery to scrape out the infection from around the kidney. He seemed to be in much more pain and more uncomfortable after this second time under the knife. He was frustrated and longed to go home. My heart ached for him, and I too wanted him to come home so we could all be together as a family. I felt helpless as I witnessed his suffering, and I longed to take away his pain and make him healthy again. I was frustrated because he had endured so much agony with the year of dialysis and the transplant, and now he had another surgery and yet more pain. I felt like asking God, "When is it enough?"

Before Joe's transplant, I had written to the fan clubs of our two favorite racecar drivers and requested a note, email, or letter to give to Joe as a gift after the transplant. Within a week of my request for an autograph, a large signed postcard arrived saying, "Get well soon — Kevin Harvick." I was so excited and impressed by the response. I hid the postcard and saved it for the transplant.

When we realized Joe would have to remain in the hospital longer than expected, I brought the precious note to the hospital.

"Hi," I said when I entered his room, where he was sitting in a chair next to the bed. "I brought you a present."

"What's that?" Joe studied the envelope when I handed it to him.

"It's something you never expected." I bit my lip with anticipation as I watched him open the large manila envelope and pull out the signed postcard.

"No way." Joe gasped and tears filled his eyes. "How did you get this?"

"I wrote to his fan club, and it arrived about a week later. I've had it for nearly a month. I thought this would be the best time to give it to you." I sat on the edge of the hospital bed. "Even Kevin Harvick wants you to get better soon."

"Wow." Joe continued to study the postcard and a smile turned up the corners of his mouth. "That is awesome."

My heart warmed when I saw Joe's expression, and I'm indebted to Kevin Harvick for the hope he gave my husband that day.

Thanks to the staph infection, Joe returned home with an open wound. Although I'm normally strong when it comes to handling medical issues, I couldn't care for the wound without feeling as if I might pass out. Thankfully, Medicare, which was available to Joe as a kidney patient, paid for a visiting nurse to care for the wound until it healed to a point where I could handle it. Zac, who was only three at the time, sat on the bed and watched while the nurse cared for Joe's wound. The nurse was reluctant to allow Zac to stay in the room, but Joe insisted. It was bonding time for Daddy and son, just like the dialysis treatments had been in the past.

Chapter Thirteen

AND BABY
MAKES FOUR

ONCE JOE'S WOUND HEALED, HE RETURNED to work full-time, and life went back to normal. Zac had his daddy, and I had my husband again. I was truly happy and so very thankful God had blessed us with good health again. I felt as if we were living a dream!

Joe was back to his usual easygoing personality too. He spent time with Zac, and we also had special couple time. It was as if we were newlyweds for the second time. We appreciated each other and all of the blessings we had in our life together.

Incidentally, Joe didn't go back to his original nephrologist after the transplant. He stayed with the group who handled the transplant. I was relieved and also a little smug because he'd finally agreed with me that it was best for him to see a different doctor.

As if things couldn't get better, Joe and I found out in August 2004 that we were expecting another child. We were ecstatic! I have to admit I was anxious throughout this pregnancy, worried that I would have another miscarriage. I fervently prayed the baby would be healthy; I couldn't imagine going through another loss.

Thankfully my prayers were answered, and the pregnancy was easy. During our prenatal visits, we found out my due date was March 29, 2005, which was the one-year anniversary of Joe's first transplant. How fitting. I was so very grateful Joe was well and we could add another child to our family.

Joe accompanied me to my obstetrician's office the day of the ultrasound. The three of us watched the screen as the ultrasound technician moved the instrument over the cool gel that had been slathered on my abdomen.

"Do you want to know the sex of the baby?" the technician asked.

"Absolutely," I said with excitement.

"Okay." She paused for a moment while moving the ultrasound tool over my abdomen. "It's a boy."

"A boy!" I grinned. "Zac will have a little brother to play with."

"That's right," Joe chimed in.

I looked at Joe. "He's going to be Matthew Joseph, and you just have to get over it. I get to name him since you named Zac."

He shrugged and said, "Okay."

Months later, on March 25, Good Friday, I began to feel contractions while I sat at home. I found a piece of paper and began writing down the times when I felt the pain. My excitement heightened as they came closer and closer together. I called my obstetrician's office, and they told me to head to the hospital.

Just my luck, by the time we got there, the contractions had subsided. I was so afraid the nurse who was examining me was going to send me home. Thankfully, however, my water broke while I was on the table, and they had to keep me. My mom and I shared a high five.

My mother and Joe were with me during the entire delivery while Zachary stayed with Joe's mother. Unlike his big brother, Matthew's delivery was easy; I pushed for only ten minutes. And Matthew Joseph Clipston didn't have to be whisked off to the NICU, as Zachary had. I had the pleasure of holding him immediately after he was born. My heart filled with warmth as I gazed into the eyes of my second child. My prayers had been answered! Zachary had a baby brother to enjoy. I was overcome by love for my family and for our new baby boy.

Matthew was born in a different hospital than Zachary, and babies at this facility were required to stay in the room with the mother, unless we requested for the baby to go to the nursery. I had to be admitted overnight, and my mother stayed with me while Joe went home to be with Zac. Matthew was asleep in a bassinet near my bed while my mother tried to sleep in a lumpy recliner.

We turned off the light in an attempt to get some rest after the long day. Once the light was off I heard snorting, groaning, and snuffling sounds from across the room.

"Mom?" I asked. "Is that you?"

"No," my mom said. "I thought it was you."

The noises continued.

"It must be Matthew!" I said before collapsing with laughter.

"He's so loud," Mom said between chuckles.

The cacophony continued for several minutes. I wondered why the sounds didn't wake Matthew up since I'd witnessed Joe's thunderous snores awakening him many times.

"I can't sleep with all of this noise," I finally admitted after my laughter subsided. "I think we need to ask the nurse to take him so we can get some sleep."

"That's a good idea," Mom agreed.

I pushed on the call button and a nurse soon appeared.

"How can I help you?" the nurse asked.

"Would you please take my baby to the nursery?" I asked while my mother snickered and my newborn continued his melody of noises. "He's really loud, and I need some sleep."

"You want me to take him?" The nurse looked stunned.

"Yes, please." I gestured toward Matthew. "I can't get any sleep with that racket."

"Oh. Okay." The nurse reluctantly pushed the bassinet toward the door. "We'll take good care of him."

Although Matthew was generally healthy at birth, his skin had a yellow hue due to a bit of jaundice. But the condition was easily cured with a few treatments under special lights. Twenty-four hours after Matthew was born, the doctor released us and we went home for Easter. Just as we had done for Zachary, we filled the initial hours with a flurry of photos, including ones of Zac holding his baby brother while sitting on a recliner in the playroom. I used my favorite shot on the birth announcements I sent out, a celebration of both of our healthy boys.

That Easter was the most wonderful and miraculous for

us. Our family was complete with our two sons and Joe's good health. We were so very thankful for all of God's blessings in our lives. Not only that, but a dear friend from church who was also Matthew's godmother snuck into our yard Saturday night and filled the lawn with plastic eggs. Zachary opened the front door Easter morning and found baskets, gifts, and toys from the Easter Bunny. Life was perfect!

Chapter Fourteen

REJECTED

UNFORTUNATELY, OUR ROAD BECAME ROCKY again eighteen months after the transplant. Matt was only six months old when Joe was admitted to the hospital with kidney rejection. The team of doctors managed it with the help of medications and treatments of plasmapheresis, which was the removal, treatment, and return of blood plasma in an effort to stop his immune system from attacking the transplanted kidney.

Plasmapheresis was pure torture for Joe, and he cried through the treatments. The plasmapheresis was administered through the pick line in his neck. His blood was cycled through a machine, and the treatments took about an hour. Joe felt a pulsating, nauseating pain, as if his head were about to explode. I sat next to him and held his hand while he sobbed.

"It's okay," I said during his fifth treatment. "You're doing great." My attempts at soothing him failed.

"I can't do this." His voice was weak through his tears.

"Yes, you can." I forced a smile despite my breaking heart. It was agonizing for me to see him suffer so much. In some ways, this was worse than the transplant and the staph infection combined.

The doctor came in and I hoped for some good news.

"How are you?" he asked.

"I can't do this anymore." Joe wiped a tear. "I feel like my head is going to explode. I can't stand it. You have to make it stop."

Tears clouded my vision as I held Joe's hand. "You're doing great." I knew my shaky tone didn't match my encouraging words. "This is saving the kidney, Joe. You have to be brave."

"I can't." His words broke into sobs that shook his entire body.

I increased my grip on his hand, hoping it would stop his body from shaking, and wiped a tear from my hot cheek while silently begging God to stop Joe's pain.

"You only have five more treatments." The doctor's expression was full of empathy. "You can do it, Joe."

"No." Joe shook his head. "Make it stop."

The doctor respected Joe's request and didn't force him to finish the last five treatments.

I kept asking God why this was happening to Joe, why this was happening to our family. Joe was the kindest and most giving person I'd ever known. I never believed that people deserved chronic illnesses, but I couldn't understand why Joe was picked to carry this burden.

And to my shame, I wondered why I'd been picked. I wondered why it wasn't enough for me to have a handicapped father who was a stroke victim. Why did I also have to have a husband with chronic kidney disease? But, although I was upset, I didn't turn my back on God this time. Instead, I begged him to heal Joe and save that precious kidney.

Chapter Fifteen

CHANGING STATES

ONE DAY, JOE CAME TO ME with a thoughtful expression.

"I think we should move to North Carolina. Charlotte."

I looked at him like he'd grown a second head. "What for?"

He'd made it through the bout of kidney rejection, and although he didn't regain full function, his kidney was working well. Life had gone back to normal, and I was thankful to have my family intact.

Joe explained that one of his friends had relocated there, and he'd heard the cost of living was lower and the opportunities were better in the automotive field.

"Are you serious about this?" I asked him.

"Yeah, I am. Why not?"

"Well, if we can take Mom and Dad, I'll go anywhere with you."

That settled it; we were on our way to a new house and new

state. Joe quickly found a job at a Ford dealership and moved in with his friend in July 2006. Since a full move couldn't happen right away, Joe traveled home on weekends and began to move boxes of our belongings into a storage unit.

I applied for jobs in Charlotte and in August managed to secure an interview for a public relations position with the City. I traveled down, praying I would somehow get this job. It was my dream to go back into the public relations field. I'd originally done that, working for the US Army Corps of Engineers. After my job was cut during a reduction in force in 1999, I'd spent the last seven years working as a technical editor in the planning division. I hoped the City of Charlotte would give me the opportunity to return to my roots. However, I was certain I bombed the interview since I felt self-conscious and goofy as I listed the reasons I was the best person for this job.

While I visited Joe, we also looked at houses. Our realtor told us the best schools were in Union and Cabarrus counties, so we spent two days traipsing through houses in those areas. None of them met our needs of having a master bedroom on the first floor with a sitting area for my father to enjoy his television without having the boys annoy him.

Worry and fear bogged my steps as we then walked through houses with all the amenities we wanted ... that were way out of our price range. I began to wonder if the move was a mistake. No one had made an offer on our house in Virginia Beach, and Joe had already left his job. It seemed like a huge risk to look at homes when we still owned one six hours away.

The day before I had to head back to Virginia, our realtor picked us up and waved around a set of plans for a house in

Union County. She explained there was a framed-up house that had a master bedroom on the first floor with a sitting area. It was perfect for my parents. The house was being constructed in an established neighborhood in an area with good schools.

We walked through and I tried to imagine what it would look like when it was fully constructed. I had a good feeling about it, and the price was affordable. The house sat on nearly an acre, which was tremendous compared to our postage-stamp-size yard back home in Virginia Beach. The boys could actually run through this yard and play without irritating any neighbors. The neighborhood had other children, and all of the houses were beautiful brick structures. A brick ranch — my parents' dream home. It almost seemed too good to be true.

"We have to make an offer on that house," I told Joe at his friend's house later that evening. "We can't let it slip by."

He angled his body toward me. "Are you sure?"

"Yes." I was suddenly filled with a sense of urgency. "The house is perfect. It has everything we need, and it's near good schools. We can't take a chance of losing it to another buyer and having to start all over again. You're already working here, so there's no stopping this train now. We're moving no matter what."

"All right. We'll do it."

Worry nipped at me as I considered this enormous decision, but I had to have faith that this would all work out. Somehow.

The following day, we sat in a restaurant with our realtor and filled out the paperwork to make an offer. My stomach tied itself into knots as we agreed to buy a house without selling our other one in Virginia Beach first. I also was agreeing to take on another house when I didn't have a job in the Charlotte area. I wondered if we were making a huge mistake. I prayed everything would fall into place, and we wouldn't find ourselves stuck with two houses and facing financial ruin.

Within a week, I received a call that I got the job at the City of Charlotte. I couldn't believe it. I was certain I'd bombed the interview, but I found out later from a coworker that I was the obvious choice for the position. The job came with a small raise, which made it even more exciting. I agreed to start work on September 11, 2006.

I naively believed I could handle leaving my children and living in Charlotte without them while we waited for our new house to be built. Zachary was starting kindergarten and Matthew was eighteen months old. I thought that since my boys were in the best care — with my mom — I would be fine.

I was kidding myself.

Being away from my children was pure torture; I ached for them. Some days I would cry at my desk when no one was around. I worried about them constantly, and I missed them. I mailed them cards filled with stickers so they would know I was thinking of them. And I traveled home with Joe every weekend to see our family and load up more boxes to take to our storage unit in Charlotte. The short visits at home were a tease and not nearly enough time with our precious children.

Our new house was delayed, and the house in Virginia Beach still hadn't sold. Things weren't going as smoothly as planned, and I again began to wonder if the move was a mistake. The financial worries of not selling our house in Virginia Beach and possibly having to pay two mortgages at once weighed heavily on my shoulders.

One evening, Joe and I went driving around Charlotte with the friends we were staying with. We stopped by a lake and I walked out onto the dock with one of our friends. I looked up at the sky and found myself wishing on a star, something I hadn't done since I was a kid. I shared with my friend that I missed my children so much that my heart hurt. I wanted them with me as soon as possible.

I increased my prayers after that night, and within a week, two families looked at our house in Virginia Beach. After worrying for so long, I felt hope and excitement well up in me at the news that someone had finally looked at the house.

I had tears in my eyes when the realtor in Virginia called to tell us the wonderful news — one of the families had offered us a contract on the house! I felt as if the pieces to our move were falling into place, and I breathed a humongous sigh of relief. Finally, some of the stress I'd been carrying around for months began to lift from my shoulders. I believe faithfulness to God's will delivered us from this difficult situation.

The family that put a contract on the house wanted to close in November, so the separation problem wasn't solved yet. I still found myself holding back tears when I was at work in Charlotte and my children were back in Virginia. I mentioned to my realtor in Virginia that having our family separated was difficult, and she said we should find a place to rent and get the family back together as soon as possible. Although my mother did not want to move twice, I insisted we find a place. I couldn't take the anguish of being apart any longer. I needed my family with me in North Carolina.

One of my coworkers offered a house for us to rent in

Albemarle. Her parents had bought the place, but then decided not to move from Cleveland. The brick ranch was the perfect temporary home. I called my mother and told her she had no choice; they were going to move down so that we could end the heartache the separation was causing for us.

We finished packing up as quickly as we could, brought the furniture and household items we needed to the rental in Albemarle, and sent the rest off with a moving company that would store it until our new house was complete.

I drove my parents, two of the four cats, and Matthew to North Carolina in our Focus station wagon. Joe took the other two cats and Zachary in the Suburban. At one point during the long trip, Joe called me.

"Do you hear this?"

In the background I could hear a cat meowing.

"Jet has been crying the entire trip," Joe explained. "Lord help me survive this without going crazy!"

I laughed. "I'm glad he's in your car and not mine." Of course, my ride wasn't a piece of cake either, but better than six hours of yowling.

The rental was smaller than we were used to, but we made it work. For the first time, the boys had to share a room, but it worked out since Matthew was still sleeping in a crib. Joe and I shared a small bedroom in the basement in order to make the upstairs comfortable for my parents and the boys. The biggest adjustment was having the washer and dryer in the basement, which meant my mother and I had to climb a steep staircase to take care of the laundry.

Halloween weekend Joe and I went up to Virginia Beach

one more time and scrubbed the house before the closing. Our last night in the house, we slept in the downstairs master bedroom on air mattresses. Tears stung my eyes as I thought of all of the wonderful memories we had formed in the house in Castleton. We had brought two babies home from the hospital there, and Zac had started kindergarten. The house held a wonderful chapter of our lives, and I would always cherish our days there. But we knew it was time to move on and start a new life in North Carolina.

We rented the house in Albemarle until we closed on our new house on December 7, 2006. Again, it wasn't easy. My mother (a saint) had to handle the commute to Zac's school in Union County—an hour each way. Poor Matthew sat in his car seat and cried for the two-hour commute. Since we weren't yet Union County residents, I had to pay tuition, which was $7 per day.

We were relieved when our house was finally complete. It was bitterly cold the day we moved, but we were home. And I breathed another sigh of relief. Life was good. Joe was healthy, and we had a new start in a new city. I couldn't wait to see what God had in store for us next.

Chapter Sixteen

DAD'S DECLINE

IN THE SPRING OF 2007, THIRTEEN years after his stroke, my father's health began to decline significantly. He spent all day in his recliner in my parents' suite watching television. He was irritable and constantly criticizing my mother's cooking or anything she tried to do for him. He also was weak and could barely walk without stumbling.

One evening Joe and I went to the elementary school to see one of Zac's programs. While we were gone, my father fell in the kitchen. My mother had to call the rescue squad to help pick my father up from the floor since he was too heavy for her to lift. When we arrived home and heard what had happened, I felt guilty for not being there to help. Thankfully, my father was okay. He had only a couple of cuts and bruises from the fall, but we knew his health was slipping. And in fact, that was the beginning of my father's decline. From then on, he fell often at all hours of the day and night. He was too heavy for Joe to lift too, so my mother had to constantly call the rescue squad.

I wished I could do something to help my mother. She was carrying a heavy burden — caring for my father and also babysitting my children. She was so stressed by how my father behaved that I worried she would have a stroke too and wind up bound to a recliner beside him.

Eventually, a doctor admitted my father to a rehabilitation center not far from our house. He spent approximately a month there, participating in physical therapy sessions and practicing how to stand and walk without falling. We had hoped the facility would be able to keep him and care for him in order to take the burden off my mother, but the doctors on the staff sent him home. My father returned home on a Wednesday, and by Friday, he had fallen five times.

"I'm at my wit's end," my mother said while she sat at the kitchen table with Joe and me one night. "I don't know how much more of this I can take."

"Did you call the rehab center?" I asked.

"I called them, but they won't help us." Mom shook her head. "The person I talked to said, 'We've done all we can for your husband.'"

"They won't do anything for you?" Joe looked appalled.

"Nope." Mom sighed.

"That's wrong," Joe said. "It's obvious that the man needs help, and it's dangerous for him to stay here. We can't handle him."

"You can't lift him," I said, pointing at Joe. "And he's getting worse. What can we do?"

"I don't know." Mom frowned, and the weight of the situation seemed to slump her shoulders.

"There has to be a solution." I prayed we would find relief for my mother and better care for my father.

One night, Mom didn't bother to wake us to tell us that my father had fallen again. Joe and I both awoke to a diesel engine roaring outside. We peeked out the front window and found a fire truck parked in the cul-de-sac in front of our house. At first we were confused, wondering why the rescue squad was in our street. But we quickly realized they must have been responding to a call placed from our home.

Frantic, we rushed downstairs and found out the rescue squad had just left our house for the second time that night. Both calls were to lift my father from another fall. Mom didn't want to wake us. Both Joe and I told her she should always call us when she needed help, and we would do all we could to help her. We didn't want her to face this harrowing situation alone.

The rescue squad came to our house again late another evening. Once again, Joe and I hurried downstairs to see what had happened. My father had fallen in front of the entertainment center in their room. My mother found him holding onto the entertainment center with blood running down his leg from where he'd scraped it.

The emergency medical technicians helped Dad get back into his recliner and took care of his wound. They also checked my father's vital signs and found his blood sugar was over 500. My father was immediately taken to and admitted at the hospital, and we found an attending doctor who understood our stressful situation. The doctor told my mother, "I don't want this for him, and I don't want this for you. He needs to go into a nursing home."

The doctor wrote orders to place my father into a nursing home. His emphysema and stroke weren't prerequisites for the nursing home admittance. Surprisingly, what got him into the nursing home was his diabetes. He was a brittle diabetic, meaning his blood sugar fluctuated, and his insulin and diet needed to be monitored by a nurse.

I had hoped to get him into a specific nursing home close to our home. I even talked to the admissions director, and she gave me pointers on how to get him admitted there. However, three nursing home admissions directors interviewed him while he was in the hospital and only one accepted him. The nursing home I'd hoped would accept him said they couldn't handle his case. I often wondered if his difficult personality was the reason they didn't choose him.

My father moved to a nursing home eight miles from our home. We had hoped to get him a private room, but he shared a room with another man. We brought him his lift chair, and I covered his dresser and window ledge with family photos in an attempt to make it cozy. His small area contained his bed, his lift recliner, a dresser, a wardrobe, and a television set. His side of the room included windows, but the shades were normally closed.

While walking through the hallways, my mother and I would see elderly people lined up in their wheelchairs. Some would say hello, some would sleep, and some would stare off into space or talk to themselves. The home also smelled putrid. Some days I would have to cover my mouth with my hand while we moved through the maze of hallways. It was sad and depressing to see my father, who was once strong, active, and brilliant, reduced to living in a place like that. Sometimes when I visited him I felt as if I were trapped in a surreal dream.

Although the adjustment was difficult, the nursing home gave my father the specialized care he needed. Dad would never allow my mother to help him with his insulin shots, and he wasn't capable of giving himself the proper dosage of the medication. He didn't follow the proper diet for a diabetic, and he wasn't the kind of man to heed advice. He insisted that the doctors were wrong, and he could eat whatever he wanted. To him, potatoes were fattening, but he ate ice cream sandwiches every night after supper. As a result, his diabetes was out of control when he was admitted, but the nurses in the home finally were able to manage his disease.

The nursing home also took some of the burden off my mother, which was a relief to me. Mom visited him three times per week and brought him clean clothes twice weekly.

Matthew loved going to the nursing home and seeing his "friends," the nurses and physical therapists who worked there. He was only two years old when my father was admitted, and Matthew would accompany my mother during her visits on Tuesdays and Thursdays while Zachary was at school. Everyone in the nursing home knew Matthew's name, and they would sometimes give him treats, such as lollipops. I believe my sweet little boy brought some joy to the dismal nursing home.

I accompanied my mother on her Sunday trips to the nursing home. I never enjoyed going, but I knew it was only proper for me to visit my father and support my mother. The visits were frustrating. I never could tell if my father truly understood me. I missed the man he was before the stroke, back when we could talk about politics and world events. The man I knew as my father was slowly drifting away. He wasn't the energetic, gregarious man I remembered from my childhood. Instead, he seemed like an elderly stranger, someone I didn't know.

Chapter Seventeen

PUBLISHING DREAMS

IN 2007 WE WERE SETTLED INTO our new home, and despite the stress of my father's declining health, we were adjusting to life in North Carolina.

Zachary enjoyed his new elementary school, and he quickly made friends. Since he wanted to be a Cub Scout, we joined the pack at our church. Joe became one of the leaders, and I helped out on the committee, assisting with events and designing a pack newsletter. Joe and I enjoyed meeting the other parents, and we soon were good friends with a few couples. I was thrilled to see Joe and Zac bond over their Cub Scout assignments and camping trips.

I was even more elated to witness my boys become play-mates as Matthew matured and became more fun for Zac.

Zachary was a veteran Fisher-Price Power Wheels driver since he had received his first motorized Jeep when he was old enough to steer. He had worn out two Jeeps before we purchased a bright green two-seater Gator. One of Matt's favorite pastimes was to sit in the Gator's passenger seat while Zac drove him around the yard and up and down the driveway. Matt happily wore sunglasses and grinned as they did laps past the garage where my mother and I sat and waved.

One warm afternoon Matt enjoyed a ride before Zac parked the Gator and moved onto another toy. When we weren't paying attention, Matthew moved into the driver's seat, and before my mother and I could stop him, he mashed down the accelerator, and the Gator sped directly toward a tree.

"Oh, no!" my mother screamed. "He's going to crash the Gator!"

"Matt!" I yelled while chasing after him. "Stop!"

To our surprise, Matthew grabbed the wheel, steered the Gator around the tree, and continued to drive as if he'd had his license for years. He wasn't yet three, but he drove around the yard with ease while my mother and I stared after him.

"He looks like a professional," I said. "I can't believe it!"

"That scared the life out of me." Mom put her hand up to her forehead. "I thought I was going to faint."

We both started to laugh as he zoomed past us again.

I shook my head in awe. "I guess he was really paying attention while his big brother drove him around."

"Just look at him! He's going to be a mechanic like his father," Mom said.

"Or a NASCAR driver." I grinned. "And I can retire while he supports me."

I enjoyed my new position with the City of Charlotte, and I slowly fell back into the groove of working in the public relations field. However, I still had a dream that haunted my thoughts — I wanted to see my name on the cover of a novel.

I had written books as a hobby since elementary school, filling notebooks with silly stories that I shared with only a few close friends. Writing was not only my creative outlet, it also was a way for me to escape stress.

After college, I joined a writer's group and learned how to polish my books. Once I was certain my book was in good shape, I began researching literary agents. After receiving enough rejections to nearly wallpaper our room over the garage in our Castleton home, I signed with an agent in 2005, and she began submitting my novel to publishers.

At that time I was writing romance novels. Although the books weren't considered part of the inspirational category, they were "sweet" romances that I felt comfortable sharing with my mother. I wrote a series of three books and then two more stand-alone novels that weren't connected directly to my series. A couple of close friends and my mother would read and edit the books before I sent them off to my agent. After my agent approved the books, she would submit them to publishers.

By the time I'd finished my fifth romance novel, I had a growing file of rejections from some prominent New York publishers. One small publisher showed an interest in one of my books and then rejected it after further consideration.

One evening after work, I sifted through the mail and found a letter from my agent. I waved the envelope as I faced my mother. "I'm not even going to bother opening this."

"Why not?" my mother asked as she sidled up to me and spotted the return address. "It's from your agent."

"I know what it is without even opening it. It's a rejection." I tossed the envelope onto the counter. "If she mails it, then it's bad news. If she calls me, then it's good news."

"You can't be sure." Mom picked up the envelope. "Want me to open it?"

"Sure." I sank into a kitchen chair while she ripped open the envelope. I watched her expression cloud as she read an enclosed letter. "It's bad, right?"

"Well." She paused. "It's not all bad."

She handed the letter to me, and I noticed that the stationery was from a prominent New York publisher. The letter was longer than most of the rejections I'd received, and I couldn't curb my curiosity. I read the letter and excitement filled me as the editor complimented the two novels my agent had submitted to her. The editor complimented my writing style and the stories, pointing out what she liked about them.

And then I read the sentence that the editor had repeated regarding both of the books: "Unfortunately, I just didn't fall in love with the story itself here."

"Typical." I dropped the letter onto the table. "Another rejection."

"Don't give up." Mom sat across from me and gave an encouraging smile that matched her upbeat tone.

"Why shouldn't I give up?" I challenged her as my voice shook with a mixture of self-pity and disappointment. "If I don't give up, then I'll just continue to torture myself with a silly dream of becoming an author. I'm obviously not good enough."

"You should keep trying because you love to write, and your agent believes in you," she said. "You can't give up now."

One afternoon in 2007, I received an email from my agent. She told me that she thought my writing showed promise, but the publishing market was changing and moving away from the romance genre I had been writing in. She asked me to try my hand at Christian fiction, and she suggested I work on a proposal for an Amish series.

Although the notion of writing something new scared me, I was intrigued by the suggestion. I felt a loose connection to the Amish since my father once told me the Amish were from the same area of Germany as his family and they spoke a dialect similar to his family's dialect. I had visited Lancaster, Pennsylvania, as a child, and I had been fascinated by Amish beliefs and lifestyle.

I'll do it, I told myself.

I pursued this project with a renewed determination to become published. I bought both fiction and academic books on the Amish and investigated the communities on the Internet. After researching everything I could find, I put together a three-book proposal, including the first three chapters of the first book in the series. I sent the proposal off to my agent in October and then continued working on the draft for the first book in the series.

Less than a month later, my agent contacted me and told me that two publishers were interested in my proposal. Although this wasn't a guarantee that they wanted to offer me a contract, it meant they were considering my proposal. This offered me a glimmer of hope that my dream might actually come true. My agent forwarded questions from the publishers. I completed the questions, then waited impatiently for more news.

After another couple of weeks, an editor at Zondervan asked to call me. I was terrified that day when we spoke on the phone, which seems funny to me now, since we have become close friends. The editor asked me if I was willing to make some major revisions to the three chapters I had submitted to her, and I told her I would do anything she suggested. I was flexible and eager to receive a chance to see my name on the cover of a published book.

On December 14, 2007, I received the coveted phone call I had always dreamt of receiving from my agent — Zondervan had offered me a two-book contract! My proposal was going to be transformed into a book, and the Kauffman Amish Bakery series was born.

Chapter Eighteen

A New Amish Friend

One afternoon in January 2008 after I received my book contract, I spoke to my editor on the phone. "Have you traveled to Lancaster, Pennsylvania, lately?" she asked.

"No, I haven't, but I went as a child. I've done a lot of research," I quickly added. "I've read as much as I could find about the Amish and Lancaster."

"You need to go there," my editor said. "You can read about it, but you really need to experience the community and the culture in order to make the details in your book authentic and also to draw the readers into your story. It would be even better if you could connect with an Amish person."

"Right," I agreed as worry filled me. "I'll do that."

I hung up the phone and slumped in my chair. I knew my editor was right. How could I write a convincing description about a place without actually visiting it?

The situation, however, was much more complicated than

simply climbing into my car and driving several hours to Pennsylvania for a leisurely research trip. How was I going to travel to Amish country and connect with an Amish person before my book's due date? Not only did I work a full-time job, but I also had two young children at home. Since the book was slated to be published in March 2009, the first draft was due to my editor in March 2008. Although I was thrilled to have my first book contract, I was overwhelmed by the writing process and the stress of handling my brand-new second job as author.

I prayed about my worries and also poured them into an email message to a dear friend whom I'd met through an online writer's group. When she replied, it was as if God opened doors right before my eyes. Not only had my friend grown up in Lancaster County, Pennsylvania, but her mother had an Amish friend!

In less than a month, I connected with Ruth, my friend's mother, and arranged to travel to Lancaster County to meet both her and her Amish friend. The details of the trip quickly fell into place and my worry eased.

With my mother as my copilot, we set off for Lancaster County in February 2008. I was excited to experience Amish country for the first time in decades, but I was also anxious about meeting my Amish friend (whom I will call Annie in order to protect her identity).

Mom and I spent a day touring Amish country with Ruth before we visited Annie. On our way to Annie's home, we spotted a market and I purchased a bag of apples as a gift for Annie, since Ruth advised me to give her something practical.

My stomach was in knots while we traveled to Annie's home. I gripped my list of questions for Annie, but I was afraid to ask anything that might be considered rude.

When we arrived, Annie invited us into her kitchen. She was a petite woman dressed in plain clothes and wearing a kerchief over her light-colored hair. She smiled and thanked me when I presented the bag of apples to her. She then invited us to sit at her long kitchen table. Annie was home with her two youngest children and also her eldest daughter, who had aged out of school. Her eldest daughter cleaned the kitchen and her middle daughter played with toys while we talked. Her youngest child was napping in a bedroom located off the kitchen.

I took in her modest home, doing my best to memorize the details of the kitchen and attempting to inconspicuously peek into the rooms nearby. The home was just as I had imagined after completing my research, but I was overwhelmed to be sitting in an actual Amish home. I was so honored Annie would allow me into her home even though she knew I was an author who wrote stories about the Amish.

Ruth and Annie talked comfortably as they updated each other on their lives and their families since the last time they had visited. I timidly asked my questions and scribbled down notes. Annie responded to them without hesitation, and soon I found she wasn't someone whom I should fear. Instead, she was soft-spoken and easygoing, and she was willing to answer anything I tossed her way.

Her middle daughter interrupted her a few times during our visit, and Annie never once raised her voice. At one point, her daughter held up a Hot Wheels toy car and said something softly in Pennsylvania Dutch. Annie leaned down and responded in their language without any sign of annoyance.

While I watched their interactions, I suddenly realized I could learn a lot from Annie. First and foremost, I could learn patience. She was the mother of seven children, but she was calm and generous with her children, even when they interrupted her. I was the mother of only two children, but I was ashamed at how quickly I would lose my patience and yell at my boys. Watching Annie, I became conscious of how I could be a better mother and also teach my children how to control their own frustrations.

I also could learn to be satisfied with what I owned. As I sat in Annie's modest kitchen, I realized my yearning for a new laptop was superfluous. Annie owned the things she needed, not everything she might have wanted. What mattered most to her was providing for her family and spending time with her precious children. I too needed to be thankful instead of greedily wishing for more expensive things.

Last, I wanted to learn how to instill the work ethic the Amish culture had imparted to Annie's children. My mother, Ruth, and I visited with Annie for approximately two hours, and Annie's eldest daughter never sat down. She continued to clean the whole time we were there. She swept the floor, moved in and out of the utility room doing laundry, and cleaned up the kitchen. Not only did she work, but she looked happy to do it! She smiled at me frequently, and the smile was genuine. I, on the other hand, couldn't ask Zachary to take out the trash without receiving an annoyed sigh and eye roll in response. I longed to have Annie teach my children the value of doing one's part to benefit the family.

After visiting in the kitchen, Annie led us outside to tour her farm. I was able to see her buggy and tour the dairy barn. I asked her several questions about the farm and continued to take notes. I took in the sights and smells while doing my best to commit it all to memory.

We were walking toward our car when a pickup truck pulled into the driveway.

"Oh, my husband, David, is home," Annie said as she waved toward the truck. "Our driver had taken him to get supplies. You'll have to meet him before you leave."

David climbed from the truck, and anxiety washed over me again. I wondered if David had known I was coming to visit. Did he approve of Annie's helping me with my research? What if he told me that I had to leave right away?

"David, this is Amy and her mother, Lola," Annie said. "Amy is working on a book about the Amish."

"Really?" David gave me a sheepish smile. "Couldn't you find something more interesting to write about?"

I chuckled at his joke, and my anxiety immediately dissolved. I never expected Annie's husband to be so warm and funny. Not only did he have a sense of humor, but he was accepting of me. The day couldn't have gone any better.

My friendship with Annie has grown immensely since our first visit in her kitchen. We moved from letters to frequent phone calls and more visits.

When I first met Annie, I was hesitant to ask her to read my books for me. Now she and one of her daughters read all of my books before they are published, and they both help me keep the story details as authentic to her community as possible.

I'm so thankful for her precious friendship. I believe God led me to write books about the Amish, and he also blessed me with a special friendship with Annie. Although Annie and I live in very different cultures, we're just two good friends when we spend time together.

Chapter Nineteen

A Prison Sentence

DESPITE THE DOCTORS' BEST EFFORTS, JOE never regained full kidney function after the rejection in 2006. The kidney, however, worked well enough to give him a normal life without dialysis. For a time. Eventually the dark cloud of kidney failure returned to our lives. In the spring of 2008, after a kidney biopsy, Joe's specialist told us the transplanted kidney couldn't be saved, and he would have to start considering dialysis and a second transplant.

I again felt as though my world was crumbling and life would never be normal for us.

Without telling me, Joe delayed the dialysis for several more months, even though his kidney function numbers, known as creatinine, showed he required it sooner. He was stubborn and didn't want to endure dialysis for the second time in his life, despite knowing he had to in order to stay alive. I was angry that he kept the news from me. He didn't want to tell me because he knew I would be upset, but I felt I had a right to know the truth, and I wanted to help him prepare for this huge change in our lives. He'd been healthy for four years, and now it was all going to change. I couldn't understand why he would choose to face this alone. After all, we'd been down this road before, and I'd done my best to be a source of strength.

When Joe underwent dialysis in 2003, he chose the peritoneal method. He decided to do the same this time, believing he'd be able to continue to work full-time as he had before. But the surgery to insert Joe's port didn't go as smoothly as we expected. When he returned to the treatment room at the hospital, he was weak — so weak that I was terrified. He couldn't stand up to go to the bathroom without my help. He leaned on me when I guided him there, and then he couldn't get back up. I'd never seen him so lethargic.

Although Joe was supposed to be released that day, I couldn't imagine bringing him home in the weak state he was in. I knew there was no way I could get him up the stairs to our bedroom. I didn't know what to do, so I explained to the nurse that Joe wasn't acting like himself. I breathed a sigh of relief when the nurse listened to my concerns, and I was thankful when she offered to help me get him admitted.

Joe spent a few days in the hospital and received blood transfusions because he was so sick. Later, the nephrologist told us that Joe's body was full of toxins due to his need for dialysis, and his body had crashed with the anesthesia. I wondered if he would have been in better shape if he hadn't delayed having the surgery and had started dialysis sooner.

Once Joe began dialysis, he tried two methods of peritoneal dialysis — dialyzing overnight with the aid of a machine and also dialyzing four times per day with the bags of saline. The cycling machine turned out to be excruciatingly painful for Joe. He would jump up out of bed with severe stomach cramping and pain. So Joe tried dialyzing himself four times a day. But unlike before, that method simply didn't clean enough of the toxins out of his body. Joe insisted he could make it work, but his doctor told him he had no choice but to do hemodialysis.

So Joe reluctantly began hemodialysis in early November of 2008. He had to go to the dialysis center in Monroe on Tuesdays, Thursdays, and Saturdays, from 6:30 a.m. until approximately 11 a.m. At first he had a port in his neck, which was called a pick line. The machine was connected directly to the port and his blood cycled back through the machine. Joe hated the port; he said it was like having a pencil stuck in his neck. He had to use special bags and wrapping in order to take a shower, and he had to be very careful not to get them dirty.

Later, he had a permanent port (fistula) surgically placed in his arm. Large needles were inserted into the fistula in order to hook him up to the machine. Again, he had to keep the fistula clean. He couldn't have any blood drawn on that arm or even have his blood pressure taken on it. As before, Joe also took a cocktail of medications to keep his blood pressure, calcium, phosphorus, and anemia regulated.

Joe hated hemodialysis. To him, it was a prison sentence. He felt as if he lost part of his life while sitting in a recliner in the center waiting as his blood ran through a giant mechanical kidney. And yet there was no other option. So for almost three years he went for dialysis three times a week. He met many other patients during dialysis. Some had given up on life and were not in good shape. Some were on government assistance and, due to their lack of insurance, weren't able to go to a transplant center. He talked about patients whose blood pressure would drop, and the nurses would have to elevate their feet.

"I think I watched a guy die today," he told me when he called one day.

I could hear the fear and anxiety in Joe's voice and shivered. "Are you sure?"

"I'm pretty sure. If he didn't die, then he's not doing too well."

"What happened?"

"The man was sitting across from me," Joe explained. "The alarms went off on the guy's machine, and all of a sudden he was surrounded by nurses."

"Oh, no." Another chill passed over me. "What did they do?"

"He must've had some sort of medical issue," Joe continued. "The nurses put screens up around him while they worked on him. An ambulance came and took him away. I'm not sure if he was unconscious or if he died."

"Did you know him well?"

"Not really, but I'm used to seeing him every time I'm here. I feel like I know him."

Although it turned out that the man was okay after a stay in the hospital, Joe worried about him until he appeared at the dialysis center again for treatments. The mental image of the man's collapse and subsequent trip to the hospital haunted me.

Although I never shared my feelings with Joe, I was concerned the same thing could happen to him.

In fact, I constantly worried about Joe during his treatments. I would check my phone frequently, awaiting a text message from him. If he called during the treatment and the tone of his voice sounded upbeat, then I knew he was having a good day. I dreaded the days when he sounded exhausted, because I knew it meant a hard day ahead for him at work. I knew dialysis would keep him alive for a long time, but I also knew the risk of complications, such as pneumonia. I prayed he would stay well and eventually have a successful kidney transplant.

One of the doctors suggested Joe continue his dialysis treatments at home. It would require a hemodialysis machine to run all night long, along with someone to stay with him to monitor his vital signs during the treatments. I found the idea preposterous. Since I was the primary breadwinner, I couldn't fathom staying awake all night with him and supervising his treatments. I had to go to work so that we could keep a roof over our heads, health insurance for Joe's condition, and food on our table.

I also didn't want the responsibility of caring for Joe throughout the treatments. I worried I would panic if his blood pressure dropped or something went wrong. What if I called the rescue squad and they arrived too late? I didn't know enough about proper medical care, and I certainly wasn't capable of knowing how to rescue him if something went wrong. It was just too much responsibility.

Joe agreed. He continued his dialysis treatments at the center, where medical professionals were available to handle any issue that might arise.

Chapter Twenty

A Terrible Loss

JOE HAD TO HAVE THE REJECTED kidney from his brother removed November 30, 2008, which was over the Thanksgiving weekend. Not only did he have to undergo invasive surgery to remove the kidney, but he had to endure the debilitating pain that followed. He was in terrible shape — walking hunched over with the aid of a cane. He spent the days after his surgery in his recliner in front of the television. I hadn't seen him this ill since he was on dialysis in 2003. Watching him suffer seemed like a terrible, never-ending nightmare.

Just when I thought things couldn't get worse, the bottom dropped out on us. The phone rang in the middle of the night of December 3. I was exhausted and, quite frankly, too lazy to answer it. Joe hobbled around the love seat where he'd been sleeping in our room and answered the phone.

He grumbled, "It's my mom. She wants to talk to you."

I climbed out of bed, sighed, and took the phone from him. "Hello?"

"Pop is dead." His mother's voice quaked.

I was fully awake in a flash, trying to process her devastating news. *Did she just say Joe's dad is dead?* "What?" I asked.

"Pop is dead," she repeated. "The police just came and told me." She choked back a sob. "I need you to tell Joe for me. I can't do it."

"What'd she say?" Joe glared at me from the sofa, frustration apparent in his expression. "What's going on?"

I couldn't answer him. I couldn't form the words to tell him the worst possible news he could ever hear — his father was gone.

I needed my mother. She could solve this for me or at least tell me how to handle it. I started down the stairs, my heart pounding against my rib cage. Joe called after me, asking what was going on, but I ignored him and continued toward the other side of the house and my mother's suite while holding the phone against my ear.

"Do you want us to come?" I asked his mother, grasping for the right thing to say. This was so unexpected. What was I supposed to do? Should we leave right now? Should we leave in the morning? My mind swirled with questions and confusion.

"I don't know right now." There was noise in the background. "I have to go."

"I'll call you tomorrow," I said before disconnecting the call.

I burst into my mother's room, and she sat up. "I need your help." I began to sob uncontrollably. "Joe's dad is dead. How do I tell him? How do I tell him? I can't do it, Mom. I can't!"

She climbed out of bed. "I'll tell him."

My mother followed me, and utter despair rained down on me as we made our way up to the bedroom.

Joe was lounging on the sofa and frowning with impatience. "What?"

Tears spilled down my face.

My mom leaned over and touched Joe's arm. "Joe, your dad is dead."

"No!" Joe bawled like a baby. "No! Not now!"

I held him while he cried. His father was his rock, his best friend. He called Joe every day to see how he was feeling. He was Joe's strength through the illness, and now he was gone. I couldn't believe it. This was so surreal and so terrible. Nothing could be worse than this, especially when Joe was so ill and needed his father's encouragement.

My mother told Joe she was sorry. I held Joe, my heart breaking with every tear he shed. I couldn't even begin to imagine the pain, but I hoped I could provide the strength he needed.

Joe and I climbed into bed, and we held hands as he fell asleep. I stayed awake for hours, thinking about his dad.

Joe's father had been living in an apartment while working in Northern Virginia. In an effort to find work, he'd taken a job as a government contractor there. On weekends, he would travel home to Virginia Beach, where Joe's mother was still living in the house they had bought in 1980 when they transferred there with the navy. Joe's father was sixty-two years old and was hoping to retire within a year.

The following morning we found out the details of what had happened. After work, Joe's father had come home and had a massive heart attack. His roommate found him when he returned to the apartment a little later.

We decided to travel to Virginia Beach the following day after Joe's dialysis. We sent Zachary to school without telling him that his grandfather was gone. I did, however, include a sealed note in his backpack informing his teacher that his grandfather had passed away and we were going to pick Zac up around 11 a.m.

I drove Joe to dialysis and then picked him up when it was over. He was distraught over losing his father and still in terrible pain from the surgery. Since Matthew was only three, we left him home with my mother.

When we arrived at the school, I left Joe in the Suburban and went in to get Zachary. My eyes filled with tears while I waited for my son to come to the office to meet me. I searched for the right words to tell him that his grandfather had passed away.

Zac looked confused when he met me outside the office. "What's wrong?"

We sat together on a bench and I touched his hand. "Grandpa had a heart attack and passed away last night." My voice shook and tears ran down my cheeks. "We're going to Virginia Beach now. I need you to be strong because Daddy is very sad. Can you be strong for me?"

He nodded. "Yeah."

We walked to the truck together, and Zac climbed into the back seat. He leaned over and touched Joe's shoulder. "I'm sorry that Grandpa died, Daddy."

The gesture touched my heart, and I studied my son with

surprise. I never imagined a seven-year-old boy could be so thoughtful and mature. I was proud of him.

The drive to Virginia was emotional. Joe broke down while talking on the phone to friends. I felt helpless, wishing I could take away his pain.

Joe's father's sisters traveled to Virginia for the service, which was planned for the end of the week. My mother-in-law's little house was full of food, friends, and family members while we prepared to say goodbye to Pop, which was what his sons and their friends called him.

We had to quickly coordinate Joe's dialysis for his stay in Virginia Beach. Joe was referred to a clinic in Norfolk that was run by one of his former doctors in the group that performed his first transplant. We awoke early on his dialysis days, and I drove him to the center where he'd have his treatment. I also picked him up and brought him back to Virginia Beach.

Friends and neighbors came to visit constantly that week. Many also came by the funeral home to pay their respects. The wake was overwhelming as the funeral home was full of old friends, neighbors, members of our former church, and friends from work. I was so thankful a few dear friends from the US Army Corps of Engineers took the time to come to the service. Their outpouring of love truly touched me.

The beautiful service was held in the funeral home. Joe's father had retired from the navy after serving twenty-two years. He had full military honors with a deafening gun salute, and the servicemen handed my mother-in-law a flag. Two of Jason's friends spoke about how much Pop meant to them and what a positive influence he was in their lives.

When the service was over, Zac burst into tears and said, "But at least we still have Poppy," referring to my father.

I hugged him and said, "Yes, that's right. We do."

Our former church, Saint Michael Lutheran in Virginia Beach, hosted a reception for us after the funeral. The women of the church donated potluck food, and tables and chairs were set up for us in the fellowship hall. It was a lovely reception, and we were so very thankful for the church's generosity.

Zac and I returned home after a week up in Virginia Beach, but Joe stayed for an extra week to help his mother sort through paperwork, clean out the apartment in Northern Virginia, and adjust to her new life. He was able to continue his dialysis treatments at the clinic in Norfolk.

The second book in my Kauffman Amish Bakery series, *A Promise of Hope*, is dedicated in loving memory to Joe's father. I will never forget what a wonderful strength and support he was to me. Sadly, although he supported my dream of becoming an author, he passed away before he could hold my first book in his hands.

Chapter Twenty-One

TIGHTENING OUR BELTS

LOSING HIS FATHER WHILE BATTLING A debilitating illness was a double whammy for Joe. His father had been his rock and a daily source of strength to him. Joe looked forward to his father's phone calls, but now those calls were gone.

I wanted to help Joe and somehow offer him love and support, but I didn't know how. I'd never lost a parent, and I couldn't fathom the depth of his grief. I shared my struggles with a friend one day on my way to work.

"I don't know how to help him," I said as our bus traveled toward Uptown Charlotte. "What can I do?"

My friend shook her head. "There's nothing you can do or say. You have to just let him work through it himself."

"Really?" I asked, hoping she could give me at least one suggestion.

"Really," she repeated. "I've lost both of my parents, and I know how he feels. There's nothing like it."

Joe went through the motions of going to dialysis and working, but even though he didn't mention it, I could see the overwhelming grief in his eyes. One night I couldn't stand to watch him suffer in silence any longer. As he sat in his recliner in our room, I sank down onto the hope chest across from him. "How are you?"

He shrugged. "Fine."

"I know you miss him."

He nodded and his eyes shone with tears. "Every day."

"Is there anything I can do for you?" I asked, hoping for an assignment, anything to make me feel like I was helping him.

"No, I don't think so." He looked at the television.

I watched him for a moment and wondered how he dealt with the pain. What helped him? How did he find his way through the grief? "Do you pray?" I finally asked.

He nodded and cleared his throat. "Yeah, I do."

"Does it help you?"

"It does." He heaved a sigh. "Every day I talk to him through my sunroof in my truck. Sometimes I yell and I cry."

"Oh." I imagined him crying alone in his truck and it broke my heart. But my friend's words echoed in my mind. I couldn't take away his pain no matter how hard I tried. "Well, I'm here if you need me, okay?"

"I know that." He gave me a sad smile. "Thank you."

Joe eventually worked through his grief, but I know he thinks of his father often. Sometimes I spot tears in Joe's eyes during special occasions or when we watch a tender movie about parents or family relationships. I know his father will always have a special place in his heart.

During Joe's hemodialysis treatment, every Tuesday and Thursday he would drive thirty-five minutes from the dialysis center to work. Frequently, he was so ill after his dialysis treatment he would arrive at work, feel terrible, and have to leave and make the journey back home to sleep in the recliner. One day he called me on the way home from work after a treatment. He asked me how I felt about his going part-time and not working on the days he had treatments. I could hear the reluctance in his voice. I knew he didn't want to ask me this, but I also knew that we had no choice. Joe had tried as hard as he could. He was finally admitting it was too much for him to endure.

I said, "I need you here. I'm not raising these kids alone. Do what you need to do."

Dread filled me after we hung up. Even though I told him to go part-time, I was terrified about how I was going to manage to pay our astronomical mortgage without his full paycheck. We'd put a healthy down payment on the house. After we closed on the home, however, Joe led me out to our large backyard and said, "This is where I will build my garage." We then took out a second mortgage so Joe could erect his dream garage with three bays for his endless car projects, including his father's 1973 Mustang coupe, a 1964 Volkswagen Beetle, and a 1964 Galaxie.

For a while we were fine with the first and second mortgages, but everything changed when Joe went back into kidney failure. The monthly bills quickly became overwhelming, and I felt as if I were sinking into a deep, dark black hole of financial ruin. Some nights I would stare up at the ceiling and wonder how I was going to manage to keep the house without a winning Powerball ticket. Some days I would close the door of my office and just weep.

We managed to refinance the house and put the second mortgage back into the main mortgage, leaving us with one huge mortgage payment for me to dread every month. Although the payment was high, it was only one payment, which seemed a tiny bit less scary than having two.

One night I sat at the kitchen table looking at a pile of bills. I grimaced as I calculated the balance in our checkbook.

"What are you doing?" Joe sat next to me.

"Trying to figure out how to pay all this. Things are tight now."

He examined the pile of bills. "I guess just pay the ones that are due now and wait until I get paid again to deal with the rest of them."

"We're going to have to cut back." I gestured toward the refrigerator. "You're going to have to start taking lunch to work, and Zac has to take lunch to school. We can't eat out all the time."

"Okay." He nodded.

"No unnecessary spending. We just have to buy the essentials right now." I hated saying it aloud since my guilty pleasure was going to the movies. I knew, however, that I could survive renting movies instead of paying to see them on the big screen.

"I got it," he said. "I'll break the news to Zac since he loves buying lunch."

Living on faith, I knew we'd make it somehow. And I knew it was a wise choice for Joe to go part-time. Looking at the bigger picture, I couldn't run the risk of him winding up in the hospital again. If he was in the hospital, he wouldn't receive any pay at all. Joe couldn't get disability insurance through work because the company said he had a preexisting condition since his kidney had already failed once. If he was admitted to the hospital, we would also wind up with another mountain of doctor bills to pay.

Still, when Joe went part-time, I constantly worried about money. At that time, he was driving from our home to a body shop located in Concord, which was thirty minutes away. He moved to a closer shop in Matthews for a few months, but then he was transferred to Gastonia, which was a fifty-three-mile commute each way. Joe drove a Suburban to work every day, which meant that half of his paycheck was going into his gas tank. We finally bought a 1992 Ford Thunderbird to try to save money on gas. That helped us out financially a little bit, but it didn't solve all of our problems.

People constantly asked me why Joe didn't go on permanent disability through the Social Security Administration. Some people insisted that being on dialysis automatically qualifies patients for disability. I suggested it to him, but Joe never pursued it. Most folks didn't understand that Joe *wanted* to work. He'd take his mind off the illness by working, and he wanted to contribute to the family. I believe staying home would have sent him into a deep depression. He needed to be around his coworkers and cars.

Having the job kept Joe going, and his employer was good to him. The company found a place for him when he was too sick to do the manual labor of fixing cars. His supervisors were flexible with his schedule. They also sent flowers and cards when he was in the hospital. The only thing we lacked was the ability for Joe to go on short-term disability insurance when he was in the hospital. I'm thankful, however, that my book royalties filled in the gaps when we needed it.

Chapter Twenty-Two

HARD TIMES

JOE WAS SO ILL SOME DAYS AFTER HIS dialysis treatment that all he did was sleep. At times he had no patience with the boys. He would snap at the slightest thing the boys did or tell them to be quiet, and I would have to bite my tongue in order to stop myself from yelling at him to pick on someone his own size.

It was tough listening to Joe correct and yell at the boys. It was worse when my mom would harp about it when I came home from work. She too was frustrated with how Joe treated the boys, but she never expressed her feelings to Joe. Instead, she would dump her frustration out on me.

"You should have seen Joe this afternoon," she'd say and then launch into whatever grievance she had for that day. "He got mad at Matt for making car noises. Honestly, what little boy doesn't make car noises?"

"Mom, you know I can't do anything about it when I'm at

work — or even when I get home." I'd sigh. "I wish you wouldn't say things like this. All it does is upset me. If you're concerned, talk to Joe."

"Well, I'm only trying to help. You should have seen Matt's face. There's no reason for Joe to get mad like that. But I won't say anything. I don't want to cause any trouble."

And there I'd be, feeling stuck in the middle. I just wished Mom would keep her opinions to herself instead of upsetting me. It was better when I didn't know everything that happened when Joe was at home and I was at work. I couldn't fix the situation, so I didn't want to get more upset by hearing how Joe had yelled at the boys. I enjoyed blissful ignorance at the office.

But to be honest, I agreed with my mom. There were days when I didn't like Joe at all and I wondered if our marriage would survive. We'd gone through a similar season earlier in his illness, but we'd weathered it and enjoyed some good years since then. Not so anymore. At this point, with Joe on dialysis again, we'd become like roommates. He had no strength left for our relationship or me. We rarely held hands or talked like we used to. I missed our little couple's dates, such as going to dinner or the movies. I missed joking around and teasing each other. I missed everything that made us a couple instead of just friends who happened to share children.

Instead, our days were spent just trying to survive the week. I was exhausted from worrying all the time and carrying the financial and emotional load for our children. I missed feeling close to Joe. I wanted to feel special again. I wanted to feel like the love of his life.

Some nights I would lie awake and listen to him snore while

wondering how everything had taken such a depressing turn. I realized my life was beginning to parallel my mother's. In 1994 when my mother was only fifty-five, my father had had his stroke. From then on, her life had revolved around my father's health. She'd had to drive him to his doctor visits, pick up his medications, and take care of all his daily needs. Because of her role as caregiver, he'd even begun calling her "Mama" instead of her nickname, "Tootie."

Now, at the age of thirty-six, I was caregiver to my husband. My existence revolved around his health. Although I didn't have to drive him to his appointments, I had to carry the load for the whole family. I not only had to take care of my children, I had to take care of my husband too. I was heartbroken that his kidney failure had stolen the very essence of what made us a couple. I felt as if I'd been robbed of enjoying the prime of our lives together. We had so many blessings, but we could not enjoy them due to his chronic health condition.

I also was offended by how friends, neighbors, family members, and acquaintances would ask how Joe was, but very few people asked how I was coping. Although I wasn't the one enduring dialysis, I was emotionally and physically exhausted from working two jobs. I was up to my eyeballs in stress while worrying about the bills, enduring Joe's moods, and trying to stay positive for the boys. There were moments when I wanted to throw my arms up in the air and say, "What about me? He would be lost without me! I'm the one supporting him and keeping it all together!"

Let's face it: I resented his illness. I wanted to live a normal life. I wanted to have date nights and family vacations. I wanted to take my kids to Disney World and make memories for them. But we couldn't do any of that. Not only were we drowning in medical bills, but Joe wasn't well enough to even go to a NASCAR race up the road in Concord, let alone make a trip to Florida.

I also regretted that we couldn't do everything the boys wanted to do because we were strapped for money and Joe was sick. I felt inferior when Zac told me about friends who played sports and went on vacations. I knew there were people worse off than we were, but I wanted to give my children more than I had when I was growing up.

The boys couldn't have friends over to play on Saturdays because Joe was so sick and cranky from dialysis that all he did was sleep. I know Zac resented that he had to go to other houses for play dates, but I didn't want Joe yelling at Zac and his friends if they were too loud. Zac also longed for a father who could throw a ball around outside and do projects with him on Saturdays. I knew my boys were missing out on special time with their father, and I prayed they would get the opportunity to enjoy their dad soon.

Zachary dreamed of going back to Cub Scouts. Joe had been his leader when he was in first grade, but those days were long gone. Now my heart broke every time Zac mentioned Scouts. I kept promising him we'd go back "when Daddy gets a kidney," but I couldn't give him a specific date that would happen. I felt powerless. I couldn't possibly volunteer to be a leader or even find time to take him to the meetings and help him with projects. I was stuck in a world of despair where I constantly disappointed my children.

At times I felt like I'd lost myself while trying to be mother, father, and breadwinner. I had no time to just concentrate on me. Some days I was both emotionally and physically spent from all of the stress weighing down on me. I was thankful for my book projects, which were my escape into a world I could control.

Still, I knew that things could be worse. Joe could have had an incurable disease, where we would only be able to cherish his remaining days together. But I knew he could live a long life on dialysis, even though it was a rough life. I held fast to my faith and believed things would get better for our family. I needed to just find patience and continue to trust God's will.

And we still had good times, which kept me going. Yes, sometimes we argued, and a few times things were so bad I wondered if we should go our separate ways. But thoughts of divorce were fleeting. Joe was my best friend and my soul mate. We were determined to make it work, no matter what, because at the end of the day, we still loved each other.

And in our darkest hours, the Lord provided. My books gave the financial, emotional, and spiritual support I needed. Not only did they help pay the mortgage, but the research brought me closer to God through the Scriptures I used in the text and the friendships I made with special readers who offered prayers for my family.

Chapter Twenty-Three

THE SEARCH
CONTINUES

WHEN JOE'S TRANSPLANTED KIDNEY FAILED, WE assumed Joe could go to the Carolinas Medical Center in Charlotte and get on the list for a new kidney. It made sense since Joe was already being seen by the Metrolina Nephrology doctor group, which operated out of CMC. We were stunned when we found out CMC didn't take our insurance. It didn't make any sense that Joe could see his nephrologist for checkups but couldn't be referred to their transplant center.

Instead, a representative from my insurance company told me only UNC Chapel Hill was considered "in network." So we had to travel two-and-a-half hours to Chapel Hill for appointments, staying overnight at a motel the night before. Even though the insurance company would reimburse our mileage, meal costs, and hotel room fees for the trips to Chapel Hill, we were beyond frustrated we couldn't go up the street from my work and register in the transplant center with the doctors Joe was already seeing for his kidney issues.

I gripped the wheel while we traveled north on Route 85 toward UNC Chapel Hill to attend an information session and complete the paperwork to get Joe on the transplant list. Joe snoozed in the seat beside me. He'd been complaining about his stomach all morning and wasn't in the mood to chitchat.

As a semi approached, I quickly signaled and merged into the center lane.

Suddenly Joe awoke and frowned over at me. "Why are you changing lanes again?"

"There's a semi coming." My eyes were glued to the mirror as the monstrous truck rumbled past.

"So?" His tone conveyed his annoyance with me. "There are always going to be semis on the road. You can't change that."

I glared at him. "My accident wasn't too long ago, and I'm still getting over my fear. You've never had your vehicle smashed by a semi, so you don't know how I feel. Have a little compassion."

"Sorry," he muttered.

I drove my burgundy Chevy TrailBlazer, the behemoth vehicle I'd bought after I was the meat in a semi sandwich. When we reached the hospital complex, I was intimidated by how close together the spaces were in the parking garage. I searched for more than one empty space so I could back in without fear of hitting another car, but found none.

I turned to Joe. "I don't think I can park it. Would you do it for me?"

"Good grief. Why did you buy this thing if you can't park it?" he grumbled. "Get out." He nearly spat the words at me.

I climbed out, and my hands shook and my growing resentment flared as I watched Joe park my large SUV with ease. When he emerged from the SUV I felt something inside me snap. I had reached my limit with his bad attitude, and I was ready to let him know how I felt.

I marched over to him. "I think you've forgotten that I've done all of this for *you*." I shook my finger in his face, completely unconcerned if we had an audience of bystanders or not. "*I* contacted the transplant department and made the appointment for the orientation. *I* booked the motel, *I* mapped the directions, *I* took time off from work, and *I* drove you here." My voice shook with my fury as I continued. "You need to realize everything I do is for you and your health. You're the focus of my life right now. I know you don't feel well, but you need to be nicer to me and appreciate everything I'm doing. I'm bending over backward for *you*."

With that, I turned on my heel and started toward the hospital building. He caught up with me, and we walked in silence while we found our way to the appropriate conference room. I was still upset, but I held my temper while hoping Joe would finally see my point of view about his behavior.

Before the appointment started, Joe leaned over and said, "You're totally right. I'm sorry."

I nodded. Although I was still upset with Joe, I felt the stress in my shoulders ease slightly. I hoped from now on he would be more mindful of my feelings and all I was doing to support him during this harrowing time.

After we spent the day at Chapel Hill, Joe's name was

entered into the system and he was put on their list to receive a cadaveric kidney. I began praying daily that he would get a call soon. Of course, I didn't want someone to die in order for Joe to receive a kidney; I just wanted a match to become available.

And then, amid all the worry and frustration, a good thing happened: my employer contracted with a new medical insurance company. This opened the door for Joe to get on the list with other transplant centers. I was grateful our prayers were answered, and that more opportunities were now available for Joe to get his health back.

We registered quickly for the list at Charlotte. I wanted to donate a kidney for Joe, so I filled out a donor packet, which included a questionnaire regarding my reasons for wanting to be a donor. One question asked if I would consider donating to someone other than my loved one. At first I checked "no," but then I read about a program called paired donation in which I would donate to a stranger in order for my loved one to receive a kidney in exchange.

A paired kidney exchange, also known as a "kidney swap," occurs when a living kidney donor is incompatible with the recipient, and so exchanges kidneys with another incompatible donor – recipient pair. Two live donor transplants would occur. For example, if there were two donor – recipient pairs, Donor and Recipient 1 and Donor and Recipient 2:

- Donor 1 would give a kidney to Recipient 2.
- Donor 2 would then give a kidney to Recipient 1.

A kidney-paired donation transplant enables two incompatible recipients to receive healthy, more compatible kidneys.

All medically eligible donor – recipient pairs may participate in the paired kidney exchange program.

I read the explanation of the paired kidney exchange program, and when I realized that my kidney donation could still get Joe a kidney, I changed my response to "yes." I would donate a kidney to someone other than Joe if it could help him in the end. I would do anything to help Joe get his health back! I filled out the questionnaire with excitement, feeling as if we were one step closer to getting Joe a kidney.

After submitting the necessary paperwork to become a possible kidney donor, I was then called in for an appointment at the Charlotte transplant center, where I had a physical, met with a social worker, and had blood work to be tested as a possible donor for Joe.

I prayed and prayed, begging God to allow me to be Joe's donor. I believed in my heart that I was going to be his match. I wanted to give him a kidney and give him life again. Unfortunately, that wasn't meant to be. The donor coordinator at the Charlotte transplant center called me and told me the news — my kidney wasn't even close to being a compatible match for Joe. She asked me to confirm that I wanted to register in the paired donor program, where I would give a kidney to someone else in exchange for a kidney for Joe, and I told her that I definitely wanted to do it. I've always believed I've been given the gift of good health and a common blood type in order to help others. I'm a regular blood donor, and I'm registered on the bone marrow list. It was God's plan for me to donate a kidney. He put the desire and courage in my heart.

Still, I was crushed when I heard I wasn't a good match for

Joe. I closed my office door and sobbed. I felt as if my world were closing in on me and there was nothing I could do. I couldn't be Joe's donor, which meant we had to wait for someone else to come forward to help him. I wanted to be his donor, and I often joked about removing a kidney with a kitchen knife and handing it to him if I could. I couldn't help thinking that if I'd been a match for him, he'd already be well. Yet I knew I shouldn't drive myself crazy with those thoughts. There had to be a reason I didn't match him, but I couldn't figure out what that reason was. Only God knew the answer.

I couldn't bear to call Joe and tell him the news that I wasn't a match for him. Instead, I called my friend at the National Kidney Foundation and cried as I told her the news. She listened and tried her best to encourage me. She also offered to be tested for him and I thanked her. I prayed she would be his best match. I called Joe next and told him the news while still crying. He told me it was okay and he was just thankful I was tested for him.

A few friends and family members also came forward to be tested. Unfortunately, none of them matched him. I deeply appreciated the generous people who were tested, and I thanked them from the bottom of my heart. But as each person was turned away as Joe's donor, my belief that I was supposed to be his paired donor became stronger. I wanted to donate a kidney for many reasons, some selfish. I didn't only want to save Joe. I also wanted to give my boys their daddy back. I wanted Joe to be able to work full-time and take some of the financial burden off me. I wanted Joe to be healthy and less moody. And I wanted my husband back. I wanted to be a couple again. I wanted us to be a family again. I wanted to take family vacations. My reasons for signing up to donate were many, but the bottom line was that I wanted Joe to be healthy.

My boys were affected by all the medical trips as well. Every time Joe went for an appointment out of town or when he was admitted to the hospital with complications, Matthew would ask if Daddy had gotten his kidney yet. He didn't understand what it meant to have a transplant. I wished it could be as easy as Matthew assumed — that we would just go to a hospital and come home with a brand-new kidney for Joe.

My mother was my rock through it all, encouraging me and helping to keep life as normal as possible for the boys. She carried the weight of the household chores while I worked two jobs. She handled the grocery shopping, the cleaning, and the laundry. When I left for work in the morning, the boys were still asleep. She got them on the bus, brought them home from the bus, and helped them with their homework. Without her, it would have been impossible to work full-time, be a mom, write novels, and care for Joe.

During this time, I knew God wouldn't abandon us. I believed Joe would get his health back. I was a relentless advocate for him, determined to find him a kidney.

And I prayed for it, begged God for it, every day.

Chapter Twenty-Four

HOPE AT JOHNS HOPKINS

IN FEBRUARY 2010, JOE AND I traveled to Johns Hopkins Hospital in Baltimore to complete testing and interviews in order to be entered into their transplant program. During the nearly eight-hour ride from Charlotte to Baltimore, the donor coordinator at UNC Chapel Hill's words echoed through my mind: "Everyone who goes to Hopkins gets a kidney. You'll have to wait longer to get one through Chapel Hill... Everyone who goes to Hopkins gets a kidney... Everyone ..." These words had become my mantra.

Once we reached the Virginia state line, we stopped at a gas station, and I offered to drive. Joe was so ill and worn out from dialysis that he slept the rest of the way. I spent the remainder of the lonely ride listening to music and praying that this trip was worth the money and time off work. We needed a miracle. We needed Johns Hopkins to finally give us Joe's life back and take the oppressive load off my shoulders.

We spent that night visiting Joe's godparents in Northern Virginia. It was fun to get caught up with them, and we talked late into the night. We stayed in their guest bedroom and I hardly slept. I was anxious for our trip to the hospital, and I prayed the visit would go well. I desperately hoped Johns Hopkins would accept me into their paired donation program, which was the key to getting Joe a kidney. The wait time and the list were much longer if he had to wait for a cadaveric kidney.

The following morning we got up around five and drove into Baltimore. Joe and I spent an entire day at Johns Hopkins visiting different teams of doctors. Joe was with the incompatible kidney transplant team, which meant that no one in his immediate circle matched him, while I was with the donation team. I endured blood work, an MRI, and interviews with a donor coordinator, transplant surgeon, and nephrologist.

The coordinator asked me why I wanted to donate a kidney. Tears filled my eyes as I gave my response. "Because I want to see my husband healthy again. I want him to be a healthy daddy to our children again."

The coordinator looked at me with sympathy.

"I just know I'm supposed to be a donor," I said. "I feel it. I must be a donor. I'll do anything in my power to give Joe his life back."

She nodded, wrote something on her clipboard. "I completely understand how you feel, Amy."

I cannot express how relieved I felt — to know that my speaking from my heart was all she needed to hear.

During the same premeeting session with the transplant team, I was told I was obese. Although at one point I had successfully made the "lifetime" designation and lost all of my required weight with Weight Watchers, I had managed to gain a good amount of it back due to the hardship of Joe's illness. I'm definitely an emotional eater and reach for food when I'm stressed.

The Johns Hopkins Hospital team accepted me into the paired donation program; however, the coordinator, surgeon, and nephrologist each lectured me about the health risks of being obese and donating a kidney.

"If you don't get healthy, you'll be at a higher risk for high blood pressure and diabetes," the coordinator said.

"I know," I said. "Diabetes and high blood pressure run in my family. My father had a stroke and he has diabetes."

"Then you already know how serious those conditions can be."

"Yes, I do." I nodded for emphasis. "I know exactly what I have to do. Weight Watchers has worked for me in the past, so I'll get back to it. I'll lose as much weight as I can while we wait for a match for Joe."

She smiled. "That's a great plan."

I was embarrassed to hear they considered me obese, but I also felt a renewed ambition to get healthy again. I wanted to be a kidney donor, and I didn't want to spend the rest of my life with health problems due to my weight. I also didn't want my children and husband to have to care for me if I wasn't healthy.

The team explained what life as a kidney donor would mean for me. I would continue to live a normal life, be able to do everything I'd always done. My only restrictions would be to avoid nonsteroidal antiinflammatory drugs (NSAIDs) and MRIs that run dye through the body, since either could be detrimental to my remaining kidney. I also needed to stay healthy, continue to watch my weight, and exercise often. And I would need yearly physicals, including blood work to check my creatinine number, the marker for kidney function.

Joe and I completed our physicals and interviews and then returned to Charlotte and our daily lives. Joe continued to suffer on dialysis and I dragged myself through work and book deadlines while praying for a miracle. A dark gloom of hopelessness hung over me, but I took solace in my fiction writing. I had no control over my life, but I could travel into the world of the Kauffman family in Bird-in-Hand and live vicariously through their trials and their joys.

One bright note was that not long after our trip to Baltimore, Weight Watchers introduced Points Plus, an updated weight loss program that provided the inspiration I needed to get back on track. I learned the new program, counted my points, and worked out nearly every day.

Some days I would call our contact at the Charlotte transplant center and see if any possible matches came up for Joe when they ran the paired donor database.

"Can you run the match program?" I'd ask.

Although I'm sure she was busy and knew what the results would be, she'd graciously comply.

"I'm sorry, Amy, but there are no possibilities listed," she'd say with regret.

"But ... there's always a possibility that you'll find a match, right?" I'd ask.

She would hesitate and then say, "Yes, there is."

But her voice was always tentative, and I was certain she was fibbing to me in order to make me feel better. Yet I held fast to that thread of hope, even if it was tenuous.

Joe's mother, Sharon, insisted on being tested as a donor during this time. She wasn't a viable donor because she was on blood pressure medicine, and kidneys help to regulate blood pressure. I had explained this to Sharon, but she still insisted she wanted to be tested. I could understand how she wanted to help her son; I would feel the same way if one of my boys needed a kidney.

So I asked my contact at the transplant center to please test Joe's mom, even though we knew she wouldn't be able to donate a kidney. My friend sent Joe's mother the testing kit, and Sharon had her blood work done. I prayed Sharon would be a good donor for Joe and that somehow the transplant would come to pass despite her need for blood pressure medication. We soon found out, however, that she wasn't a match. Joe's kidney rejection had changed the antibodies in his body, and even his mother now didn't match him. The news was a crushing blow for Sharon and also for me, but I didn't give up hope.

The wait was exasperating and some days were harder than others, especially when Joe was having a particularly tough day. However, I held onto my faith that God wouldn't lead us to Johns Hopkins and then abandon us.

Chapter Twenty-Five

LETTING GO

As if all the kidney and transplant issues weren't enough, after three years in the nursing home, my father's health began to fail again. The doctor who visited the home told my mother Dad was spiraling into kidney failure, and he recommended my father begin to have dialysis treatments. My mother refused. When the doctor seemed surprised at her answer, she explained she had watched her son-in-law, Joe, suffer on dialysis, and he was only thirty-nine years old. Dad had enough health problems, she said, and didn't need to also endure dialysis. She asked my father if he wanted to have dialysis treatments, and he also said no.

I agreed with the decision. I couldn't imagine my frail father suffering through a three-to-four-hour treatment three times a week like Joe did.

On Sunday, October 17, 2010, my mother and I left church

and went to the nursing home to see my father. He was sleeping heavily when we entered his room. Mom and I looked at each other and debated whether or not we should wake him. We decided to go by the old adage of "never wake a sleeping baby" and let him sleep.

Around 8 p.m. that evening, the phone rang, and my intuition immediately told me it was bad news. My mother answered the phone in the kitchen and then called upstairs to me.

"Poppy died," she said, using the name my children called my father.

I immediately began to sob, and I hugged Zachary, who cried along with me. Although I had known this day would come soon, I wasn't prepared for it. All of my wonderful childhood memories rained down on me, and I felt as if a hole had been punched in my chest. My dad was gone. My children no longer had a grandfather. Grief gripped me and stole my breath.

Since my mom and I couldn't bear to call my brother in New Jersey, Joe called him and told him the sad news. Eric was shocked, and he said he would come as soon as he could.

Later that evening, a neighbor came to stay with the boys while my mother, Joe, and I drove to the nursing home to get my father's things. My mother waited outside the room while Joe and I went in and filled bags with my father's clothing and personal items. Dad was still tucked in his bed and looked as if he were only sleeping. I couldn't bear to approach him, but Joe did. Leaning over my father, he said, "Tell my dad I said hello."

His words were simple, but the sentiment caused tears to fill my eyes.

While we were gathering up Dad's things, I noticed his gold

wedding band was missing. He couldn't have taken it off since his right hand was paralyzed. I mentioned it to my mother, and she asked a nurse to check the station. We were told to check with another nurse the following day.

Before we left, we talked to another nurse who expressed her condolences.

I said, "My mom and I were here earlier in the day and he was sleeping. I guess we should've woken him."

The nurse nodded. "Yes, you should've."

The woman's inadvertently cruel words stayed with me for a long time, and I wondered how things could have been different if my mom and I had woken my father. But I couldn't continue to torture myself that way. God called my father home that day, and I had no control over it.

The following day I again asked about the missing ring, to no avail. I reported the ring stolen, and a local detective ran an investigation, but the ring was never recovered. We did manage to receive a small settlement from the nursing home to compensate our loss, but it was heartbreaking to know someone stole the ring off my father's hand. My parents were married on December 13, 1958, and my father wore his ring for nearly fifty-two years. The ring can never be replaced, and it was a symbol of my parents' love for one another. I can't imagine how someone could be so callous as to steal a wedding ring from an elderly, handicapped man.

My father passed away on a Sunday, and we planned a memorial service for the following Friday. It was difficult to wait that long for closure, but it was the earliest we could have it since Joe had dialysis treatments on Tuesday and Thursday, and I wanted him well enough to stand by my side.

Friends immediately began reaching out to our family. Several brought meals to our home, and others sent cards, gift baskets, and flowers. Joe's mother, Sharon, came from Virginia for the service, along with my cousin Jeanne and her husband, Sal. My brother, Eric, also was there. We appreciated everyone's love and generosity during that difficult time.

Although I knew my father's health was failing, it was still a shock to lose him. It was surreal to plan his memorial service. I felt as if I'd lost him twice, the first time when he had the stroke and changed so dramatically, and the second time when he died.

Since we had only lived in North Carolina for four years when he died, I didn't think anyone would come to his memorial service. However, neighbors, coworkers, and many friends came to pay their respects and show their love for us. We were so touched by that.

I often wonder what life would have been like if my father never had the stroke. He would have been a wonderful grandfather to my children, and he would have celebrated my writing career with me. It warms my heart to know he would have been proud of me. I think of him every time I hold a new book in my hand.

One bright note in our sadness came a couple of days after my father passed away. My wonderful editor Becky surprised me by calling to tell me my third Kauffman Amish Bakery book, *A Place of Peace*, hadn't gone to the printer yet and there was still time to change the dedication. Just as with Joe's dad, I was able to dedicate one of my books to my father's memory.

I know my father is in a better place. His pain, suffering,

and frustration are gone, and he's a whole person again, without the disabilities that his stroke caused. But, although I know his pain is over, it's not easy to lose a parent. Milestones are especially difficult. I miss Dad when we're at our sons' music recitals, when we celebrate our boys' birthdays, and during the holidays. It always feels like someone is missing.

Sometimes Matthew still asks to visit "Poppy's house," the nursing home where my father spent the last three-and-a-half years of his life. On a more humorous note, Zac wrote an entry in his school journal that made my mother and me laugh. On the day my father died, we had adopted our cat Lily. Zac wrote in his journal: "My poppy died. But the good thing was we got a new cat."

I wish my husband and children could have known the man my father was before the stroke. I'm thankful, though, that my children have memories of my father, even though he wasn't the man who raised me. I only had the privilege of knowing my father's parents, but my children were able to know all four of their grandparents, if only for a short time. Someday my boys may tell their children about their grandparents, and they will be able to share stories about all four of them.

Chapter Twenty-Six

MY MOM AND ME

MY MOTHER AND I HAVE ALWAYS been close. She's been my best friend and confidante for as long as I can remember. When I was a child, Mom and I spent every Saturday afternoon at the movies seeing the latest matinee. I can remember the matinee prices jumping up in twenty-five-cent increments from $2.00 to $5.00 per ticket during our movie-going days.

I always felt comfortable sharing my secrets with my mom, no matter how embarrassing they were. She was an authority figure, but she was also my friend, listening without judgment and offering advice while respecting my point of view. She is an amazing judge of character and can usually figure someone out after meeting them. Mom trusted me, and if she liked my friends, she would allow me to go out with them as long as she knew where I was going to be.

For a while, I thought every mom was as cool as mine, until

I got a taste of more stuffy and strict mothers who didn't relate to their children like mine related to me. When I was in high school, one of my acquaintances called my mom the "eighth wonder of the world" because she was so fun.

When my parents moved in with us, it was as if I gained a live-in big sister. Mom and I began spending more time together. We fell into the habit of watching movies on Lifetime, Hallmark Channel, and Lifetime Movie Network whenever Joe was busy with a car project and my father was watching something that didn't interest her. We went shopping together and we shared books.

Our relationship deepened even more after Zachary was born. Mom not only was in the delivery room for the births of both my children, but she also helped care for them at home. Joe, Mom, and I took turns handling the middle-of-the-night feedings, so that we could each get some sleep. She's a second mother to the boys, and they often slip and call her "Mom" and call me "Nana" by accident.

I'm thankful that my mother has been such an integral part of my life and my children's lives. I can't imagine handling the stress of Joe's illness and working two jobs and raising my boys without her. And I believe she needs us just as much as we need her. She frequently tells people that my boys keep her young.

And since my mother and I have always been so close, watching her fall into a deep depression after my father died was heartbreaking for me. I knew losing my father would be difficult, but I never imagined Mom would take it so hard. We both knew his health was failing, and we had discussed that the end could possibly be near. I thought she was prepared. But she wasn't.

She retreated inside herself, shutting herself down emotionally. She spent a lot of time in her room and didn't want to go out of the house. I tried to coax her to go out to eat with me or catch a movie, but she said she wasn't ready. She didn't want to go out, except to take care of the boys or do her household tasks.

Out of desperation, I ordered a few books on mourning. I thought she might dismiss them as useless, so I was surprised that she read them. I also put together two framed collages of photos highlighting fun family memories with Dad. She loved them.

Her mood didn't change, however, and I was frustrated that I didn't know how to help her. I felt just as useless as I did after Joe lost his father and wanted desperately to help relieve her pain. I talked to a friend at work, who told me to give Mom space and time to go through the mourning process at her own pace. I knew my friend was right, but I hurt every time I saw my mother's sad expression. I wanted to find a way to get her out of this rut, but I didn't know what to do. The best I could do was offer a listening ear if she wanted to talk.

I called her every day from work to see how she was doing. Instead of asking her how she was directly, I would inquire about our new cat Lily, whom we had adopted the day that my father passed away.

"How's Lily?" I asked one morning while I sat at my desk at work.

"She's fine," Mom said. "She's sleeping on the sofa next to me. She's so cute."

I smiled, thankful to hear a spark of my mother's usual enthusiasm in her voice. I imagined her rubbing the cat's head while she spoke. "Lily has really fit in," I said.

"Yes, she has."

"So how are you?" I braced myself for her response. Could I handle the emotion if she cried? Would I completely lose it and cry along with her?

"I'm fine." Her tone didn't match her words.

"You sure?"

"I guess so." Mom paused for a moment. "I just feel like something's missing. It's strange not going to visit him."

"That makes sense. You had gotten used to the routine."

"And Matthew keeps asking me when we're going to go to Poppy's house."

I grimaced. "I'm sorry."

"You don't have to be sorry. He's a child. He doesn't understand."

"What can I do to help?" I offered, praying she'd give me a solution, something to make me feel useful.

"Nothing. You just have to give me time."

"Okay." Although I agreed to give her time, I hated not being able to fix this for her. I wanted to help her, but I felt lost.

Still, I found small ways to honor my father and keep his memory alive for Mom. For Christmas, I bought her a pretty memorial frame and put a photo of him in it. I also bought her a bracelet with a memorial saying and a crystal for her window. We visited his grave on his birthday in January.

After a few months, Mom finally came out of her depression, and I felt her mood lighten. She still discussed Dad, but the light was back in her eyes. I was thankful that she had come through her grief, and even more thankful for our close relationship.

Chapter Twenty-Seven

FOUND IT!

IN NOVEMBER 2010, I HAD A question about a bill we received from Johns Hopkins Hospital, and my donor coordinator put me in contact with Joe's coordinator, Nikki. Little did I know that one email regarding a bill would turn into a wonderful friendship. Nikki became a confidante, patiently answering my emails filled with questions, frustrations, and fears. She told me I could contact her as often as I needed to in order to find out the latest on Joe's possible transplant, so I would email her once a month to ask for an update. She was always pleasant and encouraging, giving me hope at a time when I had very little. Nikki was another angel in our lives.

My faith was renewed on January 8, 2011, when we found out there were two possible donors for Joe. At that point, my hopelessness turned to impatience.

That night I sat next to Joe while he watched television in

our room. "Can you believe it? After two long years of waiting we finally have two possible donors for you. We don't only have one, but we have two." I smiled at Joe. "Aren't you excited?"

"Yeah." His expression remained stoic.

"Why aren't you excited?"

He shrugged. "I don't want to get my hopes up too high. I'll be excited when I'm in the operating room waiting for the kidney."

"But this is great news, Joe. We're so much closer now than we were just a few weeks ago." I squeezed his hand. "I'm so ready for this. I'm ready to give away a kidney so that you can get one. I spent all day thinking about this. I wonder who will receive my kidney. And who will be your donor? I can't wait."

"I guess we'll see."

My mother wasn't thrilled that I was going to donate a kidney. At first she was upset when I said I wanted to be a donor, but she later understood it was the only way for me to help Joe get well again. She worried about me and all of the stress I handled during Joe's illness. She wanted that hardship relieved for me, and she knew this was the only way I could get it since I was the only donor who stuck by Joe and agreed to participate in the paired donor program.

Then one day Nikki called and shared that one of Joe's possible donors had to drop out of the program due to a health problem, and we were left with one possible donor. All Nikki could tell me was the donor was a male schoolteacher who wanted to donate during the summer. I kept wondering what the donor meant by summer. Was that June, July, or even August? When would the transplant happen? The questions haunted me, and my impatience nearly drove me insane. I would stare at my calendar and wonder on what day the transplant could take place.

For nearly three months, I prayed, begging God to make the possible summer transplant happen. I was careful to only email Nikki one time per month, even though I would've emailed her once a week if it wouldn't risk annoying her and potentially alienating her for good.

On April 3, 2011, I received an email from a contact at Johns Hopkins Hospital telling me a FedEx package with instructions for blood work was on its way to my house. My heart thudded in my chest and tears of exhilaration filled my eyes. I knew what this meant — I was going to be crossmatched with a recipient, and we were possibly moving forward with a transplant date. After praying, hoping, and crying, our kidney transplant was becoming a reality!

I completed my blood work that day, and then I prayed some more. I emailed Nikki and she told me the transplant board would meet to review our case after the crossmatch was complete between the four patients involved, meaning Joe, me, and the other two people. The day was getting closer! I couldn't believe it. My heart swelled with excitement as I posted the miraculous news on the CaringBridge website that I had set up. Supportive messages filled our page and my inbox, and I was grateful for the support and prayers from our family members and friends.

On April 14, 2011, Nikki emailed and asked if she could call me. My pulse skidded and then launched into warp speed when her phone number appeared on my caller ID. She confirmed what I had suspected — we finally had a transplant date. The wonderful date was June 14, 2011. She said she was so emotional during the transplant board meeting the night before that she cried and didn't have the emotional strength to call us. She had to wait overnight to calm herself down. She also told me that she was technically supposed to call Joe first, but she felt such a special connection with me that she couldn't wait to share the incredible news.

"I can't believe it!" I couldn't contain my joy. "This is just amazing. Can you tell me anything about Joe's donor and my recipient?"

"I can tell you that Joe's donor is your recipient's husband," Nikki said. "You and Joe match another couple."

"Oh, my goodness! Do they have children?"

"Yes, but I can't tell you anything else."

"Wow. That is just amazing." My heart warmed when I found out I was going to help another family. I was helping children get their mommy back, just as their father was helping my boys get their daddy back. The news was almost too much to bear, and I had to hold back my tears.

I asked Nikki how common it was for two couples to match. She said, "With Joe's antibodies, it isn't common." I knew then it was a miracle that we'd found a match for Joe. I was so very thankful that the donor coordinator at UNC Chapel Hill had guided us toward Johns Hopkins Hospital and our miracle.

Nikki said more information about the transplant would come to us soon through email and the mail. She asked me to call Joe and tell him.

When I called Joe with the news, he wept. He was just as surprised and happy as I was. After we hung up, I ran out into the hallway and shouted the happy news. It was finally official! We were going to get Joe a new kidney!

I felt excitement, hope, and overwhelming joy for the first time since Joe went back on dialysis. I knew God hadn't abandoned us, and now that we had a date, I had something concrete to look forward to.

I now had two more people to add to my prayer list — my recipient and the other donor. Every night I prayed for them, asking God to keep them safe and healthy. I couldn't wait to meet them. After the transplant, they would be a part of our family, our new kidney family.

Since the transplant date was now set, we began making plans. Although I wanted to have my mother with me after the surgery, I knew she was the best person to stay with our children. My mother had taken care of them since they were born, and she knew them best. She could keep them in their routine and give them all of the love and encouragement they needed while Joe and I were away.

My cousin Jeanne offered to meet me in Baltimore and stay with me during the transplant. I was thankful that she offered, since she has always been like a sister to me. Meanwhile, Joe's mother offered to be with him and take care of him after the surgery. We had our support team ready; now we just had to find a place to stay during the transplant.

Since Johns Hopkins is more than eight hours away from our home, I fretted about the logistics. The only lodging option the hospital offered was a list of hotels. When I added up the cost, I felt sick to my stomach. There was no way we could afford to spend several weeks in a hotel, especially since Joe didn't have any short-term disability insurance and wouldn't be earning any pay. I would earn only half of my regular pay through my short-term disability, and I had no way of knowing what my royalty check would be for that quarter. Feeling hopeless, I considered just putting the enormous cost on a credit card and worrying about it later, but I knew that digging us into deeper debt would only cause more anguish for me in the future.

However, once again, the Lord provided. Thanks to Facebook, I've become good friends with many of my readers. On my website, I list a PO box where readers can send a self-addressed, stamped envelope to receive bookmarks. One reader, Stacey, wrote me asking for bookmarks. She included a letter sharing stories about her Amish friends in Lancaster County, Pennsylvania. I noticed she lived in Baltimore, and I wrote to her through Facebook, sharing our story of a possible transplant at Johns Hopkins and asking if we could meet when I was in town for the transplant.

Stacey answered, and we soon became very close friends. She and her family invited us into her home during the transplant and Joe's subsequent visits to Johns Hopkins. It astounded me that she and her family would open up their home to us, since we were really only strangers. It was truly a divine blessing that Stacey and I met and became good friends. She and her family were a wonderful support to our family during the transplant, and I will be forever grateful to her for her gracious hospitality.

Chapter Twenty-Eight

FINAL PREPARATIONS

A COUPLE OF WEEKS BEFORE THE surgery, I received a call from a support person at Johns Hopkins Hospital who explained they had made a mistake when they put Joe's information into the transplant database.

"I'm so sorry to tell you this, but we entered Joe's blood type wrong."

My heart began racing as a feeling of dread filled me. The news felt like a bad dream, and I feared all was lost after we'd come so very far in the process.

"Does this mean ... Is the transplant going to be canceled?" I literally couldn't breathe as I awaited her answer.

She said no. But she also said that although the donor was a perfect tissue match, he wasn't a comparable blood type. This meant that Joe would have to complete four treatments of plasmapheresis before the transplant in order to suppress his body's immune system and prepare it to accept the new kidney.

My heart sank and I told the woman about Joe's past experience with the plasmapheresis. I explained I would have to talk gently to him about the treatments.

"I'm so sorry we didn't tell you about the plasmapheresis sooner," she said. She also apologized several times for not recording Joe's blood type correctly in her computer system. I told her there was no reason to apologize, and we would work out the logistics to get to the hospital a week earlier in order to fit in the treatments.

My stomach settled knowing that the transplant wasn't canceled, but I still was distressed. I had to somehow calmly convince Joe to endure the plasmapheresis treatments. After his experience back in 2005 — when he only made it through five of ten treatments — I knew it wouldn't be easy. But I had to find a way to convince him to endure it again or the transplant would be canceled. We couldn't do that after coming this far. I prayed he would understand why the treatments were necessary and that he would agree to do them.

Although I was tempted to call Joe at work and tell him the news, I knew it was best to wait until he got home. Once he arrived, I told him that we had to talk about something serious. He looked concerned as we sat on the sofa in the family room. I took a deep breath and explained what had happened and why he had to do the treatments, telling him that it was imperative to the transplant. He listened with a frown but took the news amazingly well. I had expected him to get upset and refuse to do the treatments. Instead he said, "Well, if I have to do it, then

I have to." I breathed a sigh of relief. We would get through this. Somehow.

Since we were slated to travel on June 7, which was Joe's fortieth birthday, we chose the weekend before to celebrate his birthday, Father's Day, and our wedding anniversary of June 20. I picked up a cake, and my mom, the boys, and I sang to Joe and showered him with gifts. Some of the gifts were practical for the transplant, such as a stack of car magazines to keep him occupied in the hospital and during his recovery. Some were fun, like the white T-shirt with a green ribbon that said "Kidney Thief" and a black shirt with green lettering that said, "I have recycled parts."

As an anniversary gift, I bought a Willow Tree statue of a man and a woman and had a special stand made with the date of the transplant added. We enjoyed our little celebration, and I looked forward to our future birthday and anniversary celebrations without the ball and chain of dialysis draining the joy and energy out of Joe. I knew bigger and better parties were in store for us.

I had asked our pastors at Morning Star Lutheran Church to include us in the prayers that Sunday before we left for the transplant. Instead of only mentioning us in the prayers during the service, Pastor John (aka "PJ") Mouritsen called us to the front of the sanctuary and said a special prayer for us. He wished my kidney Godspeed and prayed for Joe's new kidney. I was overwhelmed by the support and love from our congregation. I knew they would keep us in their prayers as we set off on our journey to get Joe healthy again.

My last day at work was the next day. I spent the time finishing up projects and submitting paperwork for my short-term disability. Before I left, a coworker brought me a bouquet of flowers and a card. When I opened the card, I gasped as I found $300 in cash. A host of my friends had signed the card and written kind words of encouragement. I was so touched and thankful. Joe and I used the money for food and gas during our trip up to Baltimore, along with a very generous Visa gift card from my friends at my publisher.

Another friend set up a meal train for us through a website. Friends from work, church, and our community signed up to bring us meals during and after the transplant. Nearly every day someone stopped by my house to give my mother another meal. We had meals stored in our large freezer for weeks after the transplant.

These were just a few examples of the angels God put in our path toward the transplant.

The day we left for Baltimore was emotional. Joe and I took the boys to school and I cried to their teachers before we left. I worried about how they would do while we were gone, and I knew I would miss them. Despite my worries over leaving them, I knew in my heart that this was the path God had chosen for Joe and me, and I believed life would improve for our children when we returned.

I prayed everything would go as planned and Joe and I would make it back to North Carolina without any medical issues or complications from the transplant. Nevertheless, in case something did go wrong, I told my mother where she could find our wills. She didn't want me to give them to her and she didn't want the code to the safe where they are kept. I knew she couldn't bring herself to consider that something might go wrong during the surgery, but I wanted to be sure all of our bases were covered in case something unexpected did happen.

We arrived at Stacey's house around suppertime. Although we had never met in person, we felt as if we'd known her and her family for years. They welcomed us like old friends. We grilled outside and sat in her garden and talked. Stacey had baked Joe a chocolate cake, and we sang "Happy Birthday" to him. The following day I had a pre-op appointment with a transplant doctor at Johns Hopkins. I had shared my weight loss journey with my donor coordinator, so she met me at the waiting area to see what I weighed when I got on the scale. I jumped up and down and cheered when the scale showed I had managed to lose thirty-seven pounds!

For the next week, Joe alternated between treatments of plasmapheresis and dialysis. The plasmapheresis treatments were necessary in order to prepare his immune system for the transplant, and the hemodialysis every other day was necessary to rid his body of toxins. To my relief, Joe did well. He said it was nothing like his first experience in 2005. I prayed daily that he would be strong enough to endure the treatments and stay healthy for the transplant. I also continued to keep my recipient and Joe's donor in my prayers, wondering if we had walked past them and not known it while we were in the hospital.

Stacey had arranged a book signing for me the Saturday before the transplant at a beautiful store called Greetings and Readings in Hunt Valley, Maryland. I hoped at least a few people would come to see me since Stacey went to the trouble to set up the event. My book signing was scheduled to begin after a well-known baseball player signed his book.

When we arrived at the bookstore, we found a line of people waiting near the table where the athlete was signing his book. The store manager explained that my book signing might be delayed because of the overwhelming response the baseball player had during his event. I told the manager it was fine since we didn't have any other plans for the day. After the manager walked away from us, Stacey poked me and then gestured toward the front of the line where a woman was holding a copy of *A Gift of Grace*.

Stacey whispered, "Those people are here for you."

I was shocked when I realized my friend was right; the line of people waiting was for me, not the baseball player. I was completely overwhelmed since I'd never had a line of readers waiting to meet me.

The event was a great success. In fact, it was possibly my best book signing in a store to date. Many of the readers who came to the signing had already heard about the kidney transplant because of my posts on Facebook. They brought gifts, offered words of encouragement, and promised to keep Joe, the other transplant couple, and me in their prayers. Their words and prayers were a comfort to me as my anxiety grew about my upcoming surgery. It was a wonderful day, and I was thankful to get my mind off the upcoming surgery.

My cousin Jeanne arrived from Virginia in time for a prayer with a minister at Stacey's church the Sunday before the kidney transplant. Joe, Jeanne, Stacey, and I went to her church and sat in a circle in the sanctuary. We talked about the transplant, and Jeanne, Stacey, and Joe shed a few tears while we discussed how much the surgery meant to us. We said a prayer, and then the minister prayed over us. That special time helped me unload my apprehension and put the surgeries in God's hands.

On Monday I was restricted to a strict clear liquid diet, including Jell-O, Popsicles, Rita's Italian Ice, and broth. Although the diet was boring, I was surprised to discover I enjoyed beef broth. Chicken broth wasn't very appetizing, but I happily drank beef broth right out of the container while dreaming of real food after the transplant.

Joe's mother, Sharon, arrived Monday evening, the night before the transplant. We took her up to the hospital to see Joe, since he had been admitted that morning in order to complete his last treatment of dialysis.

Late that evening I called my mother.

"Are you ready?" Mom asked me.

"I guess so." I sighed as I lounged on Stacey's bed. "I just can't wait until it's over. We've been talking about it for so long that I feel like it's been a lifetime since we first contacted Johns Hopkins. I just want to get through the surgery and recovery quickly."

"It will be over soon. Before you know it, you'll be home watching movies with the boys and me."

"I hope so." I stared at the ceiling. "If everything goes the way it's supposed to, I'll be home in a week."

"I can't wait. Do you want to talk to your boys?"

"Yes, please."

I heard movement and then Zachary's voice sounded through the phone. "Hi, Mom."

"Hi. Tomorrow's the big day. I just wanted to tell you to listen to Nana."

"I will."

"I love you," I said.

"I love you too. Do you want to talk to Matt?"

"Yes, please. I'll see you soon, okay?" My eyes filled with tears.

Zac handed the phone to Matt. "Hey, Mom," Matt sang.

"Hi, Matt. I love you. I'll talk to you after the surgery."

"I love you too," Matt said before giving the phone back to my mother.

"Well, this is it," I told her. "I love you. Jeanne will call you after the surgery."

"I love you too," she said. "I'll talk to you soon."

I didn't sleep much the night before the surgery. Instead, I prayed for Joe, the other couple, and me. I thought about my children and prayed for my mother. I hoped someone would periodically check on Mom and make certain she had everything she needed while we were gone. And most of all, I prayed the kidney transplants would be successful and our lives would soon return to normal.

Chapter Twenty-Nine

ALL SYSTEMS GO

As I climbed into my friend Stacey's Jeep Liberty at 4:30 on the morning of June 14, 2011, my heart raced with a mixture of fear and excitement. This was a day I'd been dreaming of for the past three years. I was going to donate a kidney to a stranger so that in exchange, Joe would receive a kidney from my recipient's husband.

Stacey steered her SUV out of her driveway with my mother-in-law, Sharon, and my cousin Jeanne following in Sharon's sedan. My bag was packed for my four-day stay at the hospital and included essentials: clothes, toiletries, a notepad, my laptop, and a stuffed cat named Kidney that my mother had bought me to be my caregiver kitty.

On the way to the hospital I talked on and on about my fears. I had insisted we leave the house in plenty of time to visit Joe before arriving at the waiting room by 5:30 a.m., the required two hours before my surgery. I wanted to see Joe one last time before we went under the knife since his surgery was scheduled after mine.

After parking, we entered the hospital and stopped by the gorgeous statue of Jesus. Visitors often rub one of the statue's toes and say a prayer, and the marble is worn on the toe from where people have rubbed it. Nearby was a book where people could write their prayers. I rubbed Jesus' marble toe and prayed for successful kidney transplants for both Joe and my mystery recipient. And I signed the prayer book, begging God to watch over all four of us and guide the surgeons' hands.

Jeanne, Sharon, Stacey, and I then hurried up to Joe's room.

"Hey!" I said as I entered the room. "Today is the day."

"Yes, it is." Joe smiled up at me.

"Are you ready?" I held his hand.

"I've been ready for three years."

"I just wanted to tell you to be good," I joked. "Don't give the nurses a hard time."

"I'll try not to." He pulled me toward him for a hug and a kiss.

"Take a good look at me because you won't recognize me after I give away one of my kidneys," I said.

He laughed and said goodbye before Jeanne, Stacey, Sharon, and I headed out of the room.

After I registered at the desk, I sat in the waiting area for a few minutes. I wondered where my recipient was and what she was doing. Was she as nervous as I was? Would she want to meet me after the surgery? What would we say to each other when we met? I didn't have much time to get lost in my thoughts before I was whisked into the back to prepare for the surgery.

Fear gripped me as I sat in the exam room, part of the holding area I call "the corral." To make matters worse, I was freezing. I was certain someone had the thermostat set to arctic. A nurse had tossed me a white gown with a blue pattern on it and told me to strip. Clad in only the flimsy gown, I shoved my clothing into the little plastic bag provided by the hospital and sat on the cold, hard examination bed while staring at the curtain. I wondered if my kidney recipient was also prepping for surgery in the same corral area.

After three long, arduous years of watching my husband suffer and carrying the emotional and financial load for my family, I'd arrived at the day I'd prayed for and dreamt of so often. Nevertheless, I was terrified to keep the promise I'd made to my family and the other couple involved in our kidney swap.

My hands shook as I thought of my mother, who was home and most likely still sleeping. It was too early to call and tell her I was prepping for surgery, but I longed to hear her voice. She was my rock, and even though I was thirty-eight years old, I wanted my mommy there with me to hold my hand before I headed into my first major surgery. But I knew my boys needed her more than I did, and I needed to be strong.

I'd had only two surgeries in my life that I felt were worthy of listing in my medical history. My tonsils and adenoids were removed in 1985, and in 2005, six months after Matthew was born, I'd had a tubal ligation, which was outpatient surgery and left me with one miniscule scar in my navel. Now here I was dressed in a hospital gown, prepping to be cut open and have a major organ removed.

The reality of what was about to happen hit me like a ton of bricks. Petrified, I wondered if I was as courageous as I had convinced everyone else I was. Was I truly brave enough to allow surgeons to cut me open and remove a vital organ? Was I courageous enough to cope with the subsequent pain? I wasn't so sure of myself anymore.

A male IV technician joined me in my teeny cubicle and began poking at my right hand to find a good IV site. I made small talk about Baltimore and how wonderful Johns Hopkins was. Instead of agreeing with me about how wonderful the hospital was, the technician complained about his job, which offered my shredded nerves little comfort. The IV stung in my right hand, but I willed myself not to cry in front of the disgruntled hospital employee. He removed the faulty IV, bandaged my right hand, and set out to find a suitable site in my left hand. After the IV was lodged in my other hand, he left.

Next, a surgeon arrived and my anxiety amplified. He pulled out a black Sharpie and drew a large "L" on the left side of my abdomen, so that the surgeons would take the correct kidney. Apparently, the left kidney is easier to place into the recipient's body. The surgeon had a thick accent, and I had a difficult time understanding the paperwork he had me sign.

Later Dr. Dorry Segev stuck his head between the curtains and said hello. He was the surgeon who would remove my kidney, and another surgeon would install it into my waiting recipient. Another team of doctors was slated to handle my husband's transplant in the afternoon.

In an attempt to keep the mood light, I asked Dr. Segev, "Could you do a tummy tuck while you're at it?"

He grinned and said, "No, I don't know how to do that."

"Oh, come on," I insisted. "You're a smart guy. I'm sure you can figure it out."

Dr. Segev laughed, and after a short conversation, he disappeared. Well, at least I had tried. As my father always said, "Give everyone a chance to say no."

Once I finished the paperwork putting my life and my kidney into the hands of the surgical team, the first surgeon left, and I was again left alone to fret over what I was about to do. I hated being alone with my worries. I wanted someone to tell me everything would be fine — that my recipient, Joe, the other donor, and I would make it through surgery with flying colors and life would be perfect after three long years of waiting.

When Jeanne, Stacey, Sharon, and Joe's transplant coordinator, Nikki, arrived, I felt my worry subside slightly. I was thrilled to finally meet Nikki face-to-face after emailing for more than a year. She and I hugged and took photographs together. I posed for more photographs with Jeanne and Stacey with my thumbs up to celebrate the momentous occasion. I also asked Jeanne to please keep my mom informed through phone calls and to have fun with my camera. She took my request seriously, and after the surgery I found photos of Joe filling out paperwork before his surgery, photos of my Facebook page on my laptop screen, and photos of Jeanne and Stacey posing with coffeepots and bottled water. They also took photos of the flat-screen board in the waiting room where my surgery was displayed on colored charts with numbers.

When it was time to head into surgery, Jeanne took my bag of clothes and my glasses. Since I'm severely nearsighted, I was nearly blind when the nurse wheeled me through the corral toward the operating room. So I closed my eyes and prayed, begging God to keep me, my recipient, Joe, and Joe's donor under his protection during the surgeries. I prayed he'd guide the surgeons' hands. And I prayed the kidneys would immediately work for Joe and my mystery recipient.

I couldn't see the nurses' faces clearly when I entered the operating room, but their voices were kind and comforting. My recipient was in another operating room nearby. My kidney would be removed, flushed, and taken to her. One of the nurses hooked up my IV, and I immediately fell asleep. The surgery, which lasted hours, was nothing but a blur to me.

Chapter Thirty

"WE DID IT!"

MY FIRST WORDS WHEN I AWOKE in recovery were, "I did it. I want a Diet Coke."

I was parched, my throat completely dry, and the nurse would only allow me tiny sips of cold water from a sponge attached to the end of a straw. When the nurse gave me a sip of water, I bit down on the sponge in an attempt to get more liquid to quench my thirst. Stacey and Jeanne both laughed. "She looks like a bird," Stacey said with a chuckle.

The recovery room was an open room clogged with beds filled with other patients, but I wasn't concerned about my lack of privacy. My only concern was that I'd survived the surgery, and from what little bits of information the nurses shared, my recipient was doing well too. God had answered my prayers, and all of the fear and anxiety I'd felt earlier had dissipated. I was in the home stretch. All I needed now was to hear that Joe was also doing well. His surgery, however, had been delayed, and no one had any information.

After a short time in recovery, a nurse wheeled me to my room with Jeanne and Stacey in tow. Sharon was in another part of the hospital awaiting news about Joe. The nurse steered the gurney into a hospital unit called the Marburg Pavilion. My room was huge and resembled a hotel room. L-shaped, it included two windows, a wardrobe, a flat-screen TV, a wooden desk and chair, a small table and two chairs, a recliner, and a large bathroom. This was unlike any accommodations I'd ever seen during my husband's numerous hospital stays since he'd been diagnosed with kidney disease in 2000. Across the hall was a family meeting room, complete with another large bathroom and shower, a kitchen area with several coffee machines, and drawers full of expensive bottled water.

My excitement about the transplant had waned during the journey to my room as the anesthesia wore off and pain set in. I felt as if I'd been run over by a Mack truck. I was hooked up to a morphine pump, so I was able to release the painkiller into my system as needed by pushing the button. When I arrived at my hospital room, a male nurse looked at the pump.

"You've pushed the button on the pump 142 times since you left recovery. Are you in a lot of pain?"

I looked at him like he was crazy. "Yes, I'm in pain." Understatement of the year.

Not only was I in pain, but I was shocked at how large my incision was. It stretched across my pelvis, similar to a cesarean. Although I knew I'd never have the body to wear a bikini, I still was surprised. I'd never asked for details about what my incision would look like, but I hadn't expected anything so severe. I also had large, colorful bruises on my abdomen which were probably from where I was held in place during the surgery.

To make matters worse, I had a catheter, along with a very unattractive drain in my pelvic area. I couldn't stand to even look at the drain, and I was thankful when it was finally removed.

Jeanne's cell phone rang and she handed it to me. "It's your mom."

"Hello?" I said, expecting to hear my mother on the other end.

"Mommy?" Matthew's little six-year-old voice rang through the phone. "I'm proud of you."

Tears flooded my eyes, and I couldn't speak. All of the emotions I'd held in since I arrived at the hospital that morning came crashing down on me like a tidal wave. I was drowning in exhaustion, pain, excitement, fear, anxiety, relief, and happiness. It was as if my feelings had been dumped into a blender and someone had mashed the button for the high setting.

My mother got on the phone, and I could tell she was crying too. Neither of us could speak. I handed the phone back to Jeanne and wiped my eyes. My mother told me later that she hadn't prompted Matthew to say he was proud of me. He'd decided to tell me that on his own.

Hearing Matthew's four simple words, I had only one thought: *This is why I donated a kidney.*

Jeanne gave me balloons with a note that said, "We love you! We miss you! You did great! Love, Zac, Matt, and Mom." I received a beautiful vase of pink roses from two of my dear friends, Sue and Lauran. Jeanne and Stacey gave me a large pink tin filled with candies and fruit. I was touched by their thoughtfulness and generosity. It was nice to know my family and dear friends were thinking of me that day.

My stuffed cat, Kidney, was also waiting for me, and I kept her by my side in bed during the recovery. As silly as it sounds, the little cat gave me comfort while I was away from home.

Joe's surgery was delayed, and he didn't get out of the operating room until later that evening. His surgery was a great success. The transplanted kidney immediately took to his body and began making urine right away. He was in such great condition that he skipped intensive care and was immediately taken to a regular hospital room. Jeanne and Stacey went to visit him after the surgery and they said he looked fantastic. I wanted to go to see him, but Jeanne and Stacey told me I should wait a day since his room was quite a trek away from mine.

Since we weren't told the name of the other couple involved in our transplants, Jeanne and Stacey had been trying to figure out who Joe's donor was. They walked through the Marburg Pavilion hallways reading the last names of the patients and the surgeons, doing their best to guess who had given Joe a kidney. When the nurse made me get up and walk, I noticed a tall man walking in the hallway and wondered if he was Joe's donor. We made eye contact, but I couldn't figure out if he was the one or not. I wanted to ask him if he had donated a kidney on June 14, but I didn't have the nerve. We passed each other without speaking at all.

The day after the transplant, Stacey and Jeanne took me to see Joe. I started out the journey pushing my wheelchair with my stuffed cat sitting in it as if she were the donor. About halfway through our trek, I had to sit in the chair. I was exhausted and still very sore from the surgery. Jeanne pushed me the rest of the way up to Joe's small hospital room on Nelson 7.

Joe's room was the typical tiny room with a small area for his bed and a teeny bathroom. My heart warmed when I saw him. I found him in his bed enduring another treatment of plasmapheresis. Even though he was hooked up to the plasmapheresis machine, he already looked healthier than before the surgery. I could tell immediately that his skin had taken on a more pink hue, and the dark circles under his eyes were fading. He was beginning to look like he did before he went back onto dialysis, and I was thrilled. I knew then my temporary aches and pains were worth it. I was so honored that I could play a part in his second transplant. All of the worrying and anguish had come to an end, and Joe had a working kidney. It was a miracle!

"Hi," I said as I sat next to his bed. "You look great."

"He's doing wonderfully," the nurse said. "He may not even need this last treatment. His numbers are great."

"Awesome." I touched Joe's hand. "How do you feel?"

"Fine. How are you?" he asked.

"Sore." I smiled. "We did it!"

"Yes, we did."

I sat in the wheelchair and talked to Joe and his plasmapheresis nurse for a while. Before we left, Stacey took a photo of me with Joe. Although it was painful for me to stand and I had very little energy, I leaned over and kissed him. It was our first kiss after the transplant. Despite my greasy hair and the fact that I was in desperate need of a bath, the photo is sweet, and I will always cherish it. The photo illustrates how our love endured his illness. We'd been down a rough road more than once, and we were still together.

Chapter Thirty-One

A FEW BUMPS
IN THE ROAD

DURING MY RECOVERY, I NEVER STOPPED thinking about my recipient. I wondered if my kidney was working for her, and I prayed she was having a good start after the transplant. I asked my donor coordinator, Sharon, and she said all she could tell me was my recipient was doing well. I wanted to meet her, and I hoped that we could work it out before we left the hospital.

Before the transplant, Joe and I were told the other couple wanted to meet us, but the news changed after the transplant. Nikki informed me the other couple didn't want to meet after all, and my heart was broken. I had dreamed of hugging Joe's donor and my recipient. I knew I would wonder about my recipient for the rest of my life, and I wanted to pray for her by name.

Three days after the transplant, Nikki came to see me in my hospital room and shared wonderful news. My recipient wanted to meet me even though her husband still chose to remain anonymous. Nikki shared that my recipient's name was Nyeisha and she was staying on the same floor as Joe was. I had a pretty box filled with copies of my books and also a white teddy bear with a green ribbon embroidered on it. Jeanne grabbed the box and Nikki led us up to Nyeisha's room on Nelson 7. While we made the trip to the other side of the hospital, excitement and anxiety filled me. I couldn't wait to meet my new kidney sister, and I wondered what I should say. I was nervous, but I was also thrilled. This was a dream come true!

I walked into her room and found her resting in bed. She was petite and pretty. We hugged and she thanked me. I met her mother-in-law, who had tears in her eyes when she hugged and thanked me. Nyeisha and I talked for a few minutes, and she shared that her kidney function was doing wonderfully.

She did, however, have some pain that didn't seem to be related to the transplant, and she was leaving in a few minutes to have tests. I gave her the gifts, and she thanked me. She also explained that her husband was shy and was nervous to meet us. She shared that he was doing great after the transplant and had already been released. I told her to please tell him thank you for us, and I told her that Joe was doing well. We exchanged addresses and phone numbers, and then I had to leave so Nyeisha could go for her tests. I promised to visit her again.

I was so excited and thankful to have met Nyeisha. I was hoping we would also meet her husband, so I could thank him in person for saving Joe's life. I was disappointed he was nervous to meet us, but I respected his decision.

Once we knew Nyeisha's name, Jeanne and Stacey were able

to figure out who Joe's donor was. His name was Eric and he was released only a couple of days after the surgery. He wasn't able to stay anonymous as he planned, thanks to an impromptu meeting one evening while Jeanne and I were visiting Joe in his room. Jeanne had stepped out into the hallway. She rushed back in and said, "Amy! Nyeisha and Eric are coming down the hallway." She motioned for me to follow her. "Come on!"

I trailed Jeanne out into the hallway and found Eric walking slowly next to Nyeisha as she pulled an IV pole. We approached them, and I was surprised to find he was the same tall man I had seen walking in the hallway after the surgery.

I walked up to him and asked, "Can I give you a hug?"

He smiled and shrugged. "Sure."

We hugged, and I thanked him for saving Joe's life. I was overwhelmed with gratitude for him. I felt as if I were meeting a superhero. He was our own personal Captain America! This was the man who had saved my husband's life, and I would forever be thankful for his generosity and selflessness.

I asked Eric if he wanted to meet Joe, and I was so excited when he said yes.

Jeanne and I led Nyeisha and Eric into Joe's room, and Joe thanked Eric and shook his hand. I was thrilled to have our kidney family together for the first time. This was the moment I'd been hoping for, and it was perfect. I was glad our meeting wasn't rehearsed. We didn't have the chance to get nervous or worry about what we would say. We were able to be ourselves and enjoy getting to know each other without any pressure.

Since Nyeisha had complications after the surgery, she was in the hospital longer than she expected. I visited her a few times before she was released, and I was able to meet more members of her family. I enjoyed getting to know her and seeing photos of her beautiful twin sons. Joe and I were at the hospital on June 27, which was the day she was released. Eric had come to the hospital to pick her up, and we were able to finally get photos of the four of us posing together. It was the last time we saw each other before we all went home to our daily routines.

While we were chatting in the hospital hallway that day, Eric said, "Joe is going to have one heck of a jump shot."

I replied, "If your wife craves Diet Coke and popcorn, that's all me."

Nyeisha and I keep in touch through Facebook, text messages, cards, and occasional phone calls. I hope someday we can get together again and our children can meet. Although she has had some health problems, her transplanted kidney has been going strong. According to the surgeon, I had a "big, beautiful kidney." I'm so grateful that my kidney is still doing its job for Nyeisha.

I cherish the photos of the four of us posing together. I have a few of the photos framed in my bedroom, our family room, and my office at work. I had several copies made and sent them to Nyeisha and also my mother-in-law. Nyeisha also has the photos displayed in her home.

When I look at the photos, I always think, "That's my kidney family." Our relationship is special and it will always be close to my heart. I love sharing our story at work when visitors notice the photos. Donating a kidney was the most rewarding accomplishment I've done in my life, other than having my children. I'm so thankful God gave me the opportunity to help another family, and I'm thankful that Eric saved my family as well.

I'd never had a major health problem in my life. Therefore, I was stunned when a nurse told me my electrolytes were out of whack and I needed medication. As a result, a technician put an IV access in my right hand. The IV burned, and I sobbed, "Whose idea was this? I just want to go home."

The doctors also couldn't find the right pain medication for me. I had a terrible reaction to OxyContin and could not eat. The doctors took me off OxyContin and tried another pain medication that gave me the shakes and made me nauseated. To stop that reaction, I wound up on antinausea medication, but I still couldn't eat. I felt terrible.

Meanwhile, Joe continued to thrive with his new kidney. The bladder apparently had to be awakened after not working for three years, so his biggest complaint was constant trips to the bathroom, a result of the kidney working well.

I'd heard that kidney donors are always in more pain than the recipients. The recipients immediately feel relief when a working kidney replaces their dialysis treatments, while the donors feel awful because they've undergone major surgery and had an organ removed. I can now attest that it's true. I felt positively horrible.

To make matters worse, my liver levels went haywire after the transplant. The doctors believed it was caused by the anesthesia. I was surprised since I'd had surgery before without any complications. The doctors told me this surgery was longer than I'd experienced in the past, and therefore a higher dose of anesthesia was used.

The doctors tried giving me another pain medication, but the liver levels still didn't return to normal. The doctors then took away my pain medications, and I had to endure horrible back pain. I wasn't allowed any medications at all, not even over-the-counter.

Sleeping was a challenge. I normally slept on my left side, but that was the side where my kidney had been removed. I had a difficult time getting comfortable, especially in the hospital bed. As a result, I was completely exhausted, which made the pain seem much worse.

I was supposed to be released three days after surgery, but the doctors kept me until June 21, watching my liver levels through daily labs. I was certain the blood work would be normal after a few days, but it wasn't. At one point, the doctors sent me for an ultrasound of my liver, and I worried they would find something terribly wrong that had been missed before the surgery. Thankfully, everything was normal on the ultrasound, and the hepatologist (liver specialist) team confirmed the rise in liver function tests was due to reaction to the anesthesia.

The days dragged on and I longed for a normal bed, a shower, and hugs from my children. I kept the stuffed cat by my side while I lounged in bed. The cat was my security away from home.

Joe's mother pushed him in a wheelchair over to the Marburg Pavilion to visit me on June 20, which was our thirteenth wedding anniversary. When he arrived, he was surprised by and a little envious of my beautiful hospital room. We took photos of him in the wheelchair and me sitting on the bed holding hands. Jeanne and Sharon then wheeled us out to the balcony overlooking the beautiful Johns Hopkins Hospital dome, and we took more photos together. It was a beautiful June day with the hot sun shining down on us. I'm certain we won't have a more unusual anniversary celebration than the one we spent at Johns Hopkins.

Although it was exhausting and hard on Joe, the pretreatments did the trick preparing his body for the new kidney. In fact, Joe was so strong after the transplant that he was released from the hospital before I was. He was able to leave on our anniversary, and I still hung in limbo, not knowing when I was going to go back to Stacey's house. I was happy he was doing so well, but I resented that he was released before I was.

I said, "This isn't fair! The donor is supposed to go home first."

Although I had some challenges after the transplant, not all of the hospital recovery was dreadful. Stacey and Jeanne took turns staying overnight in the room with me, and we had a lot of fun and laughs. They refused to leave me alone, even when I told them it wasn't necessary for them to stay. Someone was with me all the time, and I never felt lonely. I was so blessed to have two friends who acted as if they were my personal nurses. They saw me at my very worst and never abandoned me. They endured my mood swings and still continued to come back to take care of me.

Stacey almost had to endure more! The hospital bed was so lumpy and uncomfortable that I slept in the recliner one night and Stacey stayed in the bed. When a nurse came in around four in the morning to do my labs, she thought Stacey was the patient and almost drew blood from her. Stacey sat up and yelled, "No, no! I'm not the patient." She pointed to me slumped in the recliner. "She's the patient."

Since we were staying in the ritzy part of the hospital, we were able to borrow movies from the nursing station. It was sort of like a free Blockbuster store. I've always been a movie buff, so this was heaven for me. We watched a variety of movies, including some older romances such as *My Best Friend's Wedding* and some dramas such as *Mystic River*. We also enjoyed teatime at 3:30 every afternoon and became friends with the man who delivered the tea and snacks.

Chapter Thirty-Two

RELEASED

THE DAY AFTER JOE'S RELEASE I was given the go-ahead for my own. Jeanne and I packed up my things and then waited for the official paperwork. The hours ticked by and I grew impatient. I felt like an inmate awaiting her first chance to see the world outside her window after years of incarceration. I longed to sleep in a real bed without lumps, and I wanted to sleep without being awakened to have labs done in the middle of the night. Jeanne and I looked for ways to pass the time while we waited for the official paperwork that would set me free. We went out to the balcony and took more photos of the scenery. We also took photos with the nurses and the gentleman who brought the teatime snacks. Finally, I was released late in the afternoon.

When I arrived at Stacey's house, I immediately took a shower. The hot water felt heavenly. It was a blessing to finally stand in a real shower and allow the water to cleanse my aching body. I was certain I was strong enough to stand under the hot water without any help, but I soon felt weak and nearly passed out. I was so exhausted I went to bed almost immediately after having a shower. I wasn't even hungry; I just needed some rest in a comfortable bed. I could hear the loud voices of everyone visiting and talking downstairs, but I was too worn out to participate. I had a difficult time getting comfortable, but once I was able to find the perfect position on my right side, I slept until the following morning.

Friends and family members sent gifts to the house, and Joe and I were grateful for their thoughtfulness. Hundreds of friends and readers posted daily on Facebook and emailed to ask how Joe, the other couple, and I were doing. I kept them updated on our progress and asked them to keep us in their prayers since we weren't feeling healthy yet.

My Amish friend also called me after the surgery to check on me. She told me that she and her family were keeping me in their prayers. Her prayers meant so much to me, and I felt better after hearing from her. It was wonderful to know that my dear friends were thinking of me during this difficult time.

My childhood best friend, Christine, also called to check on me. She'd offered to come and see me while I was in the hospital, but her grandmother passed away unexpectedly. She was still considering making the trip from New Jersey to Baltimore, but she was having complications with her pregnancy with her second daughter. I was so touched that she was thinking of me and wanted to come visit me despite all of the trials she was facing in her own life.

My brother, Eric, took the train down from New Jersey and

visited us. I was still wiped out and very sore from the surgery, so we spent the day watching *Charlie's Angels* repeats on television. I was thankful he had come to see me. It was nice to have another family member there, especially since Jeanne had taken my car and gone back to her family in Virginia. She planned to meet up with us when we were both released and allowed to go home.

We had planned to be home within two weeks of the transplant, and I missed my children terribly. I also felt guilty that my mother had to take care of the children alone. She took the boys to a nearby aquatic center and tried to keep them busy, but she was worried about me and missed me too. At one point, while we talked on the phone, my mother admitted she was worn out from taking care of the children. I felt terrible for all she had to endure. Some days the boys did nothing but argue with each other, and I knew my mother needed some quiet time to herself.

Thankfully two of my friends offered to take both of the boys to give her a break. I was also grateful my aunt Trudy, Joe's aunt Debbie, and my friend Janet called frequently to check on my mother, and that two of our neighbors also kept an eye on her. I'm certain she was thankful for the adult conversation when friends and family called and visited her.

I was very emotional after the transplant, and I would cry frequently, which wasn't typical for me at all. I found myself bawling at the end of the movie *Valentine's Day* when Julia Roberts's character was reunited with her young son. After seeing that tender scene, I could only think of my sons and how much I missed them.

I felt as if I'd lost control of my emotions, and I was at the mercy of my tears. I never knew what was going to set me off. One day I ran into Nikki in the cafeteria at the hospital, and with tears filling my eyes, I asked her what was wrong with me. She explained that the hormonal imbalance after the transplant causes something similar to postpartum depression. The hospital had completed studies with donors, and even male kidney donors were emotional after going through the surgery. Nikki promised I would eventually feel like myself again. It took about three weeks before I wasn't crying during movies or every time I thought of my children.

While I endured my pain and emotional roller coaster, Joe had been bouncing back as if he were Superman. He was full of energy and he looked and felt great. Unfortunately, the good health was short-lived, and he managed to get himself admitted back into the hospital.

Joe had a twenty-year history of acid reflux disease. After the transplant, his acid reflux flared. In attempting to stop the pain, he took too many Tums, causing a dangerous calcium level in his body. Two doctors told him they had never seen levels that high and he set a new record for how much calcium a human can endure. I prayed his dumb stunt with the Tums wouldn't ruin what we had worked so long to achieve — life without dialysis. Thankfully, Joe was fine, but the doctors kept him at the hospital for a few days to make sure he hadn't done any damage. They pumped him full of fluids to flush out the calcium and then performed tests to make sure his kidney wasn't damaged. Although the kidney function dipped slightly, it returned to normal levels after a few days. An endoscopy found ulceration of Joe's esophagus, but it was controlled through medications.

We all breathed a sigh of relief when the doctors confirmed Joe hadn't done any damage to his precious new kidney. I couldn't imagine going through the transplant only to have Joe lose the kidney within a week.

I wasn't permitted to leave the Baltimore area due to my liver levels. My donor coordinator arranged for daily lab work, which I was able to take care of at a lab close to Stacey's house. The lab was run on a first-come, first-served basis, and we would have to sit in the waiting area and watch old sitcoms on television while we waited for my name to be called. I felt trapped. I missed my children desperately, and I wanted to go home. I had never expected I would be released from the hospital and not be allowed to leave the area, but the complications from the surgery had delayed my homecoming.

The doctors had sent me home to Stacey's house with a prescription for a pain medication that I couldn't stand to take because it made it difficult for me to go to the bathroom. Instead of suffering with the new problem, I didn't take any pain medication at all. As the days wore on, I gained more strength but was very sore. Sleeping continued to be difficult. I asked if I could go home and follow up with lab work there, but the doctors wanted me to stay in the immediate area since the liver level issue had them stumped.

Sharon, the donor coordinator, called me early one morning while I was staying at Stacey's house and Joe was still readmitted at the hospital. "How are you feeling, my dear?" she asked.

I promptly burst into tears. "I want to go home!"

"I know you do, Amy. But we must make sure your liver levels are back to normal before we can let you travel home."

"But I miss my boys," I whined. "I need to see them!"

Her voice became stern. "You have to wait until you're well enough to go home."

"I know," I snuffled. I knew she was right, but I didn't want to hear it. All I wanted was my children. I missed them so much that my heart hurt.

Sharon told me to take it easy, explaining that my liver issues were contributing to my exhaustion. Now, that was advice I was happy to take. Aside from daily blood draws and visiting Joe in the hospital, Stacey and I spent a lot of time relaxing on her comfortable La-Z-Boy recliner sofas and watching movie after movie. I am thankful that I was able to concentrate on recovering since Joe's mother, Sharon, spent her days at the hospital with Joe after he was readmitted. Stacey spent her days with me since she is a schoolteacher, and she was off work for the summer. I can't remember the long list of movies we watched, but we enjoyed our lazy time.

On June 24, my literary agent, Mary Sue Seymour, came to visit me. She had come to town since one of her sons lives in Baltimore and had recently bought a house there. Since Joe was still in the hospital, Stacey and I picked up Mary Sue and took her to the Café Hon, a well-known restaurant in the area. We had a wonderful time talking with Mary Sue, and she brought me a bag of gifts. I was so touched that Mary Sue took the time to see me and brought me such thoughtful and generous gifts. I was worn out after the visit but happy that I was able to get out and do something fun.

Joe was released from the hospital for the second time on June 29. Meanwhile, two of my three liver levels had returned to normal, and the doctors expected the third to return to normal shortly. I no longer had to go for daily labs, and my donor coordinator told me I could leave the area. Finally, after nearly three weeks away, we were free to go home.

I was elated! Joe and I decided to surprise our family and not tell them we were coming home. We couldn't wait to see the shock on their faces when we pulled into the driveway the following day.

Chapter Thirty-Three

THE HOME STRETCH

WE WERE ON OUR WAY HOME at last. Since Jeanne had gone home to Virginia on June 22 in my car, we planned to meet her at a Cracker Barrel in Ashland, Virginia, to pick up my vehicle. I was sad to leave Stacey and her family, but I also couldn't wait to see my boys again. It had been too long. I felt as if I'd been gone for six months instead of only one.

We squeezed in a quick trip to Toys R Us to pick up some special gifts to bring home to our boys, then left early the following day and headed south. Excitement filled me when we got on the road. I couldn't wait to see my boys' faces! They would be so surprised to see us, and we had a load of Captain America toys to excite them even more. I drove with Stacey in her Jeep, and Joe and his mother followed in her car. The traffic was backed up and it felt as if it took forever to get from Stacey's house to the Cracker Barrel off of Route 95.

Jeanne was waiting for us at the restaurant, and I was happy to see her again. We had breakfast and then moved my luggage from Stacey's Jeep to the trunk of my little Honda Accord coupe. (I'd given up my TrailBlazer for a smaller, more economical car in the spring of 2011.) That taken care of, we stood in the parking lot and said our goodbyes. I hugged Stacey, and both of us had tears in our eyes before she left. I thanked her again for hosting our family, and I also thanked Joe's mother, Sharon, for giving up nearly a month of her life to take care of Joe at the hospital.

I then climbed into the driver's seat of my car, excited to be behind the wheel for the first time in nearly a month. Poor Jeanne was cramped in the tiny back seat and barely had enough room to sit beside the piles of pillows and gifts for the boys we had crammed in beside her. Jeanne never complained. Instead, she insisted she was comfortable. Joe snoozed in the passenger seat beside me.

I had lied to my mother and told her we didn't know when we were going to be able to go home, but we were certain it would be possible for us to leave in a few more days. It was difficult keeping the fib going all day. One time she called and I told her I was sitting in Stacey's house watching television, even though I was in reality driving my car toward home. Another time I had to get her off the phone as quickly as I could because Jeanne was talking to her family on her cell phone in the back seat. My mother knew Jeanne had gone home on June 22, and she would've figured out I had been lying to her if she knew Jeanne was with me again. Jeanne put a pillow in front of her face in order to prevent my mother overhearing the conversation. It worked, and my mother didn't suspect a thing.

My excitement swelled the closer we got to home. My mother called while we were within a few miles of the house. She shared that one of my friends who rode the bus with me was bringing a meal and a neighbor was going to pick up Zachary and take him out to eat at McDonald's. She moved onto mundane things, and I kept the conversation short, telling her Stacey and I were watching a movie and planning supper. She believed me, which was shocking since I'm not a very convincing liar, and my mother knows me well. I'm surprised she didn't suspect anything when I hurried her off the phone once again.

I thought I might burst with excitement when I saw my brick house at the end of our street. The car trip had lasted twelve long hours. It seemed surreal — after enduring the kidney transplant and all of the complications, we had finally made it home. I couldn't wait to see my children, my mother, and my cats. We were home at last!

When we pulled in the driveway, I laid on the horn, tooting it repeatedly to announce our return. My mother was standing at the front door with my friend Gaye, who was delivering a meal for the family. I could tell by my mother's expression that she was confused. Since she wasn't expecting us, she didn't recognize my car. She stared at the vehicle and said, "Who on earth is that blowing the horn?"

I jumped out of the car and said to my stunned mother, "Don't you know my car?"

Zachary rushed across the front yard and hugged me. He then hugged Joe and sobbed in his arms. He had missed us tremendously, and all of the emotion came pouring out in his tears.

I hugged my mom, who continued to look surprised and

confused. "You told me you weren't coming home for a few days!" She laughed. "You lied to me."

"Yes, I did," I said, laughing too.

Jeanne smiled. "I was hoping you couldn't hear us in the car. It was hard not to laugh when Amy talked to you on the phone."

I asked my mother where Matthew was, and she told me to go to the front door and knock. He had gone into the house to get a snack.

Eager to see Matthew, I hurried to the front door and knocked.

He came to the door and looked confused. "Mom? Is that you?" he asked as he opened the door. "Mom!"

"Yes, it's me!" And then he hugged me. My heart swelled with joy. I was so happy to be home.

Jeanne snapped photos through the whole thing. I'm so thankful that she captured our surprise homecoming. The photos show the shock on my mom's and Matthew's faces, and Zachary crying with joy in Joe's arms. There were also photos of me posing with the boys and our neighbors talking to Joe.

Matthew and Zachary had created colorful posters for us and hung them in the garage in anticipation of our return. One poster said, "Welcome home! We missed you!" Matthew had drawn stick figures of himself and me. The other poster said, "Thank you, Jeanne!" The posters were a sweet gift for our homecoming, and we were all touched by them.

Joe visited with the boys and our neighbors in the driveway for a while and then helped me give the boys their gifts. I'll never forget the excitement and happiness we felt that day. It was so very wonderful to finally be home.

Unfortunately, the homecoming wasn't completely without

stress. Against my mother's and Jeanne's advice, I went through our mail and found a basketful of medical bills the day after we arrived home. Most of the bills were overdue since we'd been gone nearly a month. The bill that sent me spinning into despair was a $1,600 deductible for dialysis.

I sobbed while going through the bills, even though my mother told me I was pushing myself too much. Another bill was an overdue notice for a personal property tax on my Chevy TrailBlazer, which we'd sold months earlier. I cried and carried on when I couldn't find the receipt that would prove we didn't owe the tax money. Thankfully, Joe felt well enough to go to the City and handle the issue right then. He found the appropriate person at the tax office, and it was cleared up quickly. The bill was disregarded, and we didn't owe any money at all.

Normally the bills wouldn't have gotten me so upset, but I was exhausted and still in pain from the transplant. It was all overwhelming on top of not feeling strong.

Jeanne and Joe stayed for the long holiday weekend. The boys enjoyed Jeanne's company and played games and ran around the yard with toy guns. They were sad to see her and Joe leave again. But on Tuesday, July 5, they headed back north. Joe needed more testing and a checkup on his progress, and Jeanne needed to go home. I worried about Joe while he drove alone, but he was fine. I called him frequently to check where he was, and he arrived when expected at Stacey's house. Joe's health was even better than the transplant doctors had anticipated, and he was able to return home July 15.

I had blood work on July 5, and it showed that my remaining liver level was finally coming down to where it needed to be. Although the level wasn't back to normal, Sharon, the transplant coordinator, told me I was allowed to take Tylenol. I was thrilled since Tylenol was what I had craved all along. Thanks to the medicine, I could finally get comfortable enough to sleep at night.

I slowly regained my strength and felt like myself again the week of July 18. I spent as much time with the boys as I could before returning to work, taking them to movies and the local aquatic center. I also managed to finish line edits that week for my book *Reckless Heart*, an Amish young adult novel. The boys, my mother, and I had a wonderful week, and I was glad to do a few fun things with them before I had to go back to the daily routine at the City of Charlotte.

I returned to work on Monday, July 25, exactly six weeks after the transplant. While my pain and exhaustion lasted for five weeks after the transplant, Eric, Joe's donor, was playing basketball and winning every game by week four. I couldn't even imagine shooting hoops after six weeks. But I was glad I didn't have any long-term problems with my liver, and I was happy I would not have to return to the lab for blood work for six months.

Life was finally getting back to normal.

Chapter Thirty-Four

BACK WHERE
WE BELONG

PERHAPS THE MOST IMPORTANT PART OF Joe's transplant and recovery was the fact that he could be a real dad again. After years of being too ill to participate in our boys' lives, he was once again taking part in all the things he'd loved and missed out on. And the boys flourished under his care.

In August, Joe took the boys to the Outer Banks for a long weekend to visit Jeanne and her family. The boys were thrilled to go to the beach, and Jeanne sent me wonderful photos of them playing on the beach with her sons and their girlfriends. Part of me wished I could've gone with them, and I felt as if I was missing out on all of the fun while I sat at my desk at work. On the other hand, I was happy the boys could have a mini family vacation for the first time in a long time. And one with their dad.

In July 2010, I had taken the boys with me to Disney World for the Romance Writers of America conference. Joe had stayed home because he had to continue his dialysis, and as he always said, it's not fun to be sick in a hotel room. I'd missed Joe while we were in Disney World, and I wished he could be there to see the excitement on the boys' faces as we toured the amusement parks. I was happy he could take the boys to the beach and they could enjoy his presence after watching him suffer on dialysis for so long.

Glad he could finally take care of some of the projects he'd longed to do while he was on dialysis, Joe painted two hallways in our house and completed some small home improvements. I was elated to see him up and moving again. I had my healthy, active husband back again.

Joe took twelve weeks off after the transplant and then returned to work. It was a relief to have him working full-time again. I knew he felt good to be contributing more to the family, and I felt less of a burden financially. I no longer had to stare at the ceiling on sleepless nights and worry about the bills.

Zac had had to quit Cub Scouts when Joe went back on dialysis in 2008. However, in the fall of 2011 we joined a Cub Scout pack as a family, with Matt starting as a Tiger Scout and Zac as a Webelo. It was both rewarding and comforting to go to Scouts as a family. In the fall of 2012, Joe became Matt's Wolf Pack leader. What a miracle that was, to see him once again leading one of his sons!

And not only were the boys able to do things with Joe, but they were now able to do things in general. Before, because of the constant care Joe needed, we simply didn't have time for extras. Now the boys were able to take music lessons, with Zac playing guitar and Matt learning drums.

While Joe was sick, I couldn't always do the things with the boys that they wanted to do, such as taking them out to ride their go-carts. I didn't know enough about the go-carts to even start them, much less hook the trailer up to the Suburban, load the go-carts, and take them to a track. When the boys asked to ride the go-carts, I had to tell them to wait until Daddy felt well enough to help them. I could see the disappointment in their eyes, but I had to say no. There were also times when the boys asked me to help them build or fix something, and I was useless. Again, I hated telling them no, but there was nothing I could do, except pray Joe would get better and be able to be the father he wanted to be. And, thankfully, our prayers were finally answered!

The boys enjoyed having their daddy back. They spent time with him while he worked on cars in the garage, and they also gave him little projects to do for them. For a while, Joe spent quite a bit of time painting special Lego characters for the boys. He also helped Zachary build and paint model cars. It warmed my heart each time I saw Joe involved with our boys.

Since Joe no longer had dialysis on Saturdays, he was also free to do things he wanted to do. And I could run errands without dragging the kids along with me. It was easier for me to plan book signings and speaking engagements because I knew Joe would be available to spend time with the boys. I previously felt guilty for planning anything on a Saturday since my mother would be stuck with the boys after having them all week. Now I could do things with friends or my mother on a weekend without feeling guilty. I enjoyed my newfound freedom as much as Joe did his!

Joe and I were able to spend more time as a couple now, and our intimacy was restored. I no longer felt like just a roommate. There was no more resentment at having to carry all of the burdens. Instead, I felt like Joe's partner. We joked around and laughed like we used to before he got sick. We enjoyed date nights and not having to worry about whether Joe would feel well enough to go. It was a blessing to be a normal, healthy couple, and I was so grateful to feel close to Joe again.

I am still grateful.

Part of me cringes at the thought of using the old adage "It was all worth it." The pain and fear. The uncertainty and disappointment. The stress and anger. The roller coaster of ups and downs partnered with two transplants. But in the end it *was* worth it. The journey toward getting Joe healthy was long and arduous. At times I believed the nightmare would never end. At times I just wanted out of it all. The difficult times, however, transformed into blessings. Our marriage — our family — is stronger now, and this long journey has helped me realize what's most important in my life: my loved ones and my faith.

Epilogue

ALTHOUGH JOE HAS BEEN HEALTHY SINCE the kidney transplant, we still live and die by his precious creatinine numbers, which are the markers for his kidney function. Normal kidney function is between 0.9 and 1.2. He has monthly lab work, and I always hold my breath when he calls me to tell me the results. His numbers have been staying between 1.0 and 1.2, which is in the perfect, healthy range. In the back of my mind, however, I fear that something can go wrong. I never imagined we'd have the first kidney transplant, and never in my wildest dreams did I believe we'd have to go through a second, more difficult transplant.

I keep Joe and Nyeisha on our prayer list at church. Every week I submit the same prayer: "Continued kidney health for Joe and Nyeisha." Joe once told me that he doesn't need to be on the prayer list anymore, but I disagree. I don't think we should ever stop praying for his or Nyeisha's kidneys.

I've often joked that I asked for a thirty-year warranty on his new kidney, but the reality is that there is no guarantee and no warranty. My childhood best friend Christine's father gave his sister a kidney in the late 1970s when we were only children. Her aunt's transplanted kidney lasted thirty years, and her transplant took place before all of the modern technology that was available when Joe received his first transplant in 2004. I was certain that since Christine's aunt's kidney lasted so long, Joe's first transplant would too. It shocked me when Joe's first transplanted kidney lasted barely four years. I pray Joe and Nyeisha have the blessing of a long, long life with their new kidneys, just as Christine's aunt did.

Although I try my best not to live with a black cloud of worry shadowing me every day, I do feel that fear in the back of my mind. That is part of the reason I would never dream of walking away from my day job and my health insurance. If Joe carried our health insurance, we'd lose it if he could no longer work. I know I shouldn't live with the fear of the kidney failing, but it's already happened to us once. I can't pretend it couldn't happen again.

What scares me most about the possibility of Joe losing his new kidney is that I have nothing left to give him. I couldn't be his donor and help him get into the paired donor program again. I could only provide his health insurance and stand by his side as his wife. And if he did lose this kidney, I would pray someone would come forward to be a donor for him. Hopefully a special person would see how healthy Jason and I have been since donating a kidney, and they would consider giving Joe the same gift that we gave him.

I don't, however, dwell on the negative or live in a place of fear. Joe's second kidney transplant was truly a miracle, and I'm thankful for all of the wonderful angels who came forward to help us through those three long years while we waited for a kidney match. I'm thankful for friends, neighbors, and readers who offered words of encouragement through email messages, text messages, and cards, and I'm thankful for those who offered their encouragement in person. I'm grateful for the friends who brought us meals or called to check on us during the transplant. I'm grateful for the wonderful staff members at Johns Hopkins Hospital who took care of us. To this day, we keep in touch with our coordinators, Joe's local doctors, and the dialysis technicians at the center, who are all blessings to their patients.

I truly believe Joe and I went through this second transplant for a reason, to be an inspiration to others. Joe and I have weathered the storms of his illness and become closer. Since he was diagnosed with kidney disease in 2000, we've seen many of our friends divorce. Although we had some rough times, we stayed together, and neither of us would consider walking away from each other after all of these years. We don't get stuck on the petty arguments; we look at the bigger picture and work through the rough times.

Joe was an inspiration to the patients and nurses at the dialysis center. He stayed positive throughout his illness and never gave in to depression. Even though he could have gotten disability, he stayed active and continued working. His strength has inspired others. He has spoken to patients who are on dialysis and considering a transplant, and his warm and caring personality has made him a wonderful support and mentor for those patients.

I'm honored I was able to give a kidney and help a woman get her life back. I'm humbled God gave me this opportunity, and I hope our story is an inspiration for my children and my readers.

One lesson I learned through the kidney transplant is that we couldn't plan anything. Since both Joe and I had complications, our plans changed by the day, sometimes by the hour. Yet in the end, everything turned out the way it was supposed to — Joe regained his health and I recovered from my complications.

The transplant took place in God's time, just as many people told me it would, and it was wonderful and beautiful. I look forward to many, many years of enjoying Joe's good health. And I plan to keep him and Nyeisha on my prayer list throughout every one of those blessed years.

ACKNOWLEDGMENTS

As always, I'm thankful for my family, including my mother, Lola Goebelbecker; my husband, Joe; and my sons, Zac and Matt. I'm blessed to be surrounded by your love. Thank you, Joe, for allowing me to share our journey toward your second kidney transplant. I'm honored you chose me as your life partner, and I'm thankful I could be a part of your kidney journey. We make a great team.

Thank you to Nyeisha and Eric for allowing me to tell the world about our story. I'm so grateful God brought our families together to form our new kidney family. I'm honored to have been a part of our paired donor exchange. You'll continue to be in my prayers and my thoughts daily.

I'm more grateful than words can express to my patient friends who critique for me — Stacey Barbalace, Margaret Halpin, Amy Lillard, Janet Pecorella, Lauran Rodriguez, and, of course, my mother. I truly appreciate the time you take out of your busy lives to help me polish my books.

Thank you also to my dear friend Pam Smith. I enjoy our lunchtime walks and discussions. I appreciate your willingness to listen to me and offer encouragement for my writing projects.

I'm so thankful for all of the wonderful people at Johns

Hopkins Hospital who made our transplant a reality. Special thanks to Nikki Lawson, renal transplant nurse coordinator; Kate Knott, transplant nurse practitioner; and Sherrie Klunk, living kidney donor evaluation coordinator, who helped with the details for this book. You are all a blessing to your patients!

I'm grateful for my cousin, Jeanne Lampropoulos, who stayed by my side during the transplant. You're the sister I never had! I'm so grateful to have you in my life. Love you!

Joe and I will always be indebted to Stacey, Keith, and the rest of the Barbalace family. You all were a tremendous help to us, and we're grateful for your generosity and hospitality. Your family welcomed us into your home, giving up bedrooms to make room for Joe, Sharon, Jeanne, and me. We were blessed to be able to stay with you and enjoy all of the comforts of home within thirty minutes of the hospital.

Thank you to my mother-in-law, Sharon, who stayed by Joe's side during the transplant. We appreciate the time you took to stay with us in Baltimore, and we couldn't have made it through the transplant without you.

I'm grateful also to Joe's godparents, Alan and Mary Beth Hemer, for their love and support during the kidney transplant. We'll never forget your generosity. We're so thankful to be a part of your family.

I'm thankful for the wonderful team at Metrolina Nephrology who are working hard to keep Joe and other kidney patients well. Special thanks to Holly Garner, FNP-C, for your help researching Joe's health history and providing details for this book.

Thank you to my wonderful church family at Morning Star

Lutheran in Matthews, North Carolina, for your encouragement, prayers, love, and friendship. You all mean so much to my family and me.

To my agent, Mary Sue Seymour — I am grateful for your friendship, support, and guidance in my writing career. Thank you for encouraging me to pursue telling my story.

Thank you to my amazing editors — Sue Brower and Becky Philpott — for believing in this book and guiding my words. I appreciate your guidance and friendship. You're a blessing in my life! Thank you also to Leslie Peterson for helping mold the first draft of this book into something that someone might actually want to read. I'm grateful to each and every person at Zondervan who helped make this book a reality.

To my readers — thank you for choosing my books. My books are a blessing in my life for many reasons, including the special friendships I've formed with my readers.

Thank you most of all to God for giving me the inspiration and the words to glorify you. I'm so grateful and humbled you've chosen this path for me.

BLOOD AND ORGAN DONATION

I BECAME A BLOOD DONOR WHEN I was sixteen, inspired by my mother who donated blood frequently when I was a child. I remember my mother coming home with "Be nice to me, I gave blood today" stickers on her shirt. She donated blood in memory of a boy who once lived next door to us. His name was Jimmy, and he was diagnosed with leukemia when he was little.

While Jimmy was suffering from leukemia, he would come and visit me while I sat in a playpen on our back porch. The other children in the neighborhood would taunt him, but he found peace when he came to see me. My mother told me Jimmy would visit with me for hours. He even gave me a pet rabbit that I named Ballerina Bunny, and he would bring me toys when he came home from his treatments.

Tragically, Jimmy passed away on March 7, 1977, when he was only ten years old and I was four. I began to give blood in memory of him as soon as I was old enough to donate. I was very young when he was alive, and therefore I don't remember him. I do remember the stories about him, and I kept his photograph on my dresser throughout my childhood. I'm also registered to donate bone marrow in memory of Jimmy, and I hope someday I can help someone like him by giving my bone marrow. I dedicated my book *Reckless Heart* to Jimmy's memory. Even though I don't remember him, he had a profound effect on my life, and he will always live in my heart.

After Joe received six units of blood within six months, I was inspired to share our story. I contacted the person who was in charge of the blood drive committee at work and asked if I could compose an email to share with the six thousand employees of the City of Charlotte in order to try to recruit more people for the bimonthly blood drives. The Community Blood Center of the Carolinas (CBCC) heard about our story and then confirmed that Joe had received the blood from its organization. Our family is featured in one of CBCC's brochures and on their website to encourage folks to donate blood. We also were featured in a video that shares stories of patients who have benefited from blood transfusions.

I now am a part of the blood drive team at work, and I also run the blood drives at Morning Star Lutheran Church. Blood donation is one of my passions, along with organ donation. I've experienced firsthand how blood donation can save a life, and I'm determined to encourage others to donate blood. I donate every fifty-six days, and my blood goes to ill infants and babies through a CBCC program.

If you have never donated blood, you can attend a nearby blood drive or contact your local blood bank or the Red Cross to find out how to make an appointment. Blood donors need to be healthy, at least seventeen years old, and at least 110 pounds. At your appointment, a medical professional will go over your health history and conduct a brief examination to measure your temperature, pulse, blood pressure, and hemoglobin (or hematocrit). You may be deferred if you show symptoms of cold or flu, if your iron level is low, if you are taking certain medications, or if you have traveled to certain countries. For more information, a full list of eligibility requirements, and tips for a successful donation, see *www.redcrossblood.org/donating-blood.*

Of course, because of Joe's kidney issues, Joe and I also are active with the local National Kidney Foundation and played a big part in their Blue Jean Black Tie fundraiser on May 8, 2009. I've spoken at the National Kidney Foundation's Cadillac Golf Classic and other meetings, and my family and I participate in the annual Kidney Walk. A simple way you can contribute to the cause of organ donation is by simply signing up to donate your organs in the case of your death, and also to encourage other family members to do so. You can go to *www.organdonor.gov* to register or ask at your local Department of Motor Vehicles.

I hope that this book can highlight the importance of blood and organ donation. These intimate donations of flesh and blood are not only a gift of love; they are for many people a precious gift of life.

THE HEARTS OF
THE LANCASTER GRAND HOTEL

"Clipston's series starter has a compelling drama
involving faith, family and romance."

—*Romantic Times* 4 1/2-star, TOP PICK!
review of *A Hopeful Heart*

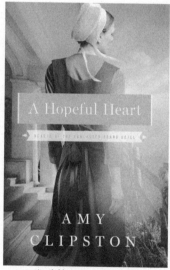

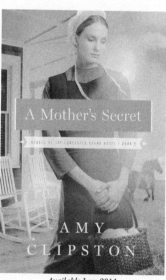

Available as print and e-book   *Available June 2014*